Miss Great Britain

1945-2020

The Official History

Sally-Ann Fawcett

2QT Limited (Publishing)

First Edition published 2020 by

2QT Limited (Publishing)
Settle
North Yorkshire
BD24 9BZ

Cover design by Richard Wendt at richardwendtdesign.co.uk
Cover images: supplied by author with permissions
Photographs are copyright and with kind permission from :
Lancaster City Council; Tom Wren (Creative by Wren); Brian Hayes Photography; Jin Rathod Imagery;
Pukaar News; Trevor Adair; Rubicon Photography; Paul Carroll (Monsignor Photography)

Printed in the UK by Lightning Source UK Ltd

A CIP catalogue record for this book is available
from the British Library

ISBN 978-1-913071-79-0

Foreword

It is typical that the first Miss Great Britain pageant I ever watched as a child was one of the most controversial.

It was 1975, and Susan Cuff was announced the winner, only for some of the other contestants to flounce off the stage in a huff. The high drama mixed with dazzling glamour sealed it for me, and Miss Great Britain instantly became one of my favourite pageants.

It is therefore an understatement to say that when the Miss Great Britain office emailed me, out of the blue, in 2014 to ask if I would like to join the judging panel, it was something of a dream come true.

They had seen my book, *Misdemeanours: Beauty Queen Scandals,* and thought I would be suitably qualified to join the panel. I was quaking in my stilettos to sit with the likes of Duncan Bannatyne, of *Dragons' Den* fame, that night, but it was a fabulous experience, and to my delight and honour I have been invited back, as Head Judge, ever since.

I love Miss Great Britain: it is one of the most inclusive pageants in the country, with no restriction on marital status, background, shape, size or height. And now with the new title of Ms Great Britain, no upper age restriction, either.

My attempt to record and celebrate seventy-five years of the longest running pageant in the country has been a true labour of love, and I have some very special people to thank who helped me achieve this:

Morecambe Business Improvement District for their support in my documentation of some of Morecambe's recent history, of which Miss Great Britain played such a huge part.

Donald West, a pageant historian from Canada, who gifted me, with incredible kindness, a huge back catalogue of Miss Great Britain programmes dating back to the 1940s. I could never have written this book without such staggering generosity.

Kate Solomons-Freakley and Jemma Simmonds, directors of the Miss Great Britain pageant and two of the kindest, most genuine people I have met, for inviting me to judge their fabulous pageant every year since 2014 and for including me in so much of their decision making and ideas. I am truly blessed to have met them.

Trevor Adair, Amanda Dyson, Sally Gillborn, Susan Cole, Susan Berger, Pat McIntosh, Laura White and the late and sadly missed Sophie Gradon, for sending me priceless photos and mementos from the pageant, and for speaking to me about their experiences. They have all added so much to this book and I can't thank them enough.

This book is dedicated not just to the amazing women who have worn the crown and clutched the silver rose bowl with such pride, but to every single one of the thousands upon thousands of young ladies who have come from every corner of Great Britain to compete, and who are part of the history of this incredible pageant that began beside a rain-swept lido seventy-five years ago.

Thank you, ladies: you have all made history.

Sally-Ann Fawcett

Also by the author:

Misdemeanours: Beauty Queen Scandals

More Misdemeanours & Other Beauty Queen Stories

Mis-3-meanours: Second Runner-Up

1945

When the *Sunday Dispatch* newspaper joined forces with Morecambe & Heysham Corporation to create a new tourist attraction for the town in 1945, few would've bet more than a shilling that it would still be going strong seventy-five years later.

But Miss Great Britain celebrated its Diamond Anniversary in 2020 and has cemented its status as the country's longest-running beauty pageant.

When recalling its history, it is little mentioned that Eric Morley was instrumental in the origins of the Miss Great Britain pageant and that this, not his Miss World contest that came six years later, was his first foray into the beauty queen business.

As publicity officer for Mecca, the huge dance hall and bingo entertainment group, Morley agreed that heats of Miss Great Britain should take place in his dance halls, thus bringing in new audiences to his venues, as well as giving the pageant some instant prestige.

But on 29th August 1945 there were no such luxurious surroundings for the contestants of the very first Miss Great Britain pageant, or the National Bathing Beauty Contest, as it was called then. Watched by a crowd of 4,300 people, the finalists paraded round the lido in a continuous downpour.

Morecambe's Super Swimming Stadium opened in 1936 and was said to be the largest outdoor pool in Europe. It had been built in direct competition with Blackpool's South Shore Swimming Coliseum, which was a decade older. The Stadium provided the perfect backdrop for the first National Bathing Beauty Contest and remained so until the site's closure in 1975 and subsequent demolition.

As Charles Eade, editor of the *Sunday Dispatch*, explained, 'Britain was at war at the time and many of her loveliest girls were in the Services, but we decided to run a contest that year on modest lines and test the public's reaction. Male members of the Forces were known to have more than a passing interest in "pin-up girls" so it was agreed to let them judge the preliminary heats.'

The first heat was held at the Swimming Stadium on 25th July 1945, and Mary Drummond, a nineteen-year-old from Glasgow, was the winner. There were only five heats that year, but public interest was so great that a total of 5,700 turned up to watch them that summer.

Lydia Reid, a local girl from Morecambe, made history by becoming the first winner of the famous silver rose bowl, but she nearly hadn't made it to the final at all. She had taken part in the last of the weekly heats, but when she wasn't announced as one of those going through to the final the crowd, mainly consisting of airmen fresh home from the war, went mad and noisily demanded a recount.

Officials held a hasty consultation and they wisely decided not to disappoint their armed forces heroes, overturning the decision; Lydia was through.

There was no need for a recount a week later: Lydia, a typist for the civil service, was the outright victor, and proud winner of no less than a seven guineas cash prize and a swimsuit.

That very first title was contested by five other finalists: June Rivers of Manchester, Alice Tolley of Blackpool, Mary Drummond from Glasgow, Doreen Roper of Chesterfield, and Lancaster's Jeanne Dunster.

The judging panel consisted of film star Michael Rennie, Norman Craig, the divisional publicity manager of the Gaumont British Corporation, and Denis Shipwright of Gainsborough Pictures.

In an interview with *TV Times* sixteen years later, Lydia – by then a married mother of three living in Felixstowe – recalled those days with great affection and amusement.

'Even buying a bathing suit back then was difficult as clothing coupons were so precious,' she said. 'Luckily, my mother was a dressmaker and was able to run up a swimsuit for me out of a piece of white satin.

'I only entered the contest for a bit of devilment,' she continued. 'Then the lads kicked up such a fuss when I wasn't picked for the final!'

Lydia went on after her reign to win a *Health & Strength* contest, and was invited back by the Miss Great

Britain organisers in 1968 as a special guest judge. What surprised her was not just the inflated prize money on offer of £2,000 – 'I was born out of my time!' she laughed – but how much more seriously the modern contestants took the competition.

'When I was in it I walked around the pool like a carthorse, treading on everyone's toes, and I did my own hair, too. Now all the outfits and hairdos look so expensive.'

And something that wasn't repeated by the 1968 winner was Lydia's method of celebration. 'When I won I leapt off the stage and into the pool,' she said. 'I got told off when I climbed out because my hair was all wet and they hadn't taken a photograph of me looking all nice!'

Lydia Reid, first National Bathing
Beauty Contest winner in 1945

1946

Manchester's June Rivers returned a year later to take the second National Bathing Beauty Contest title 1946, beating eight other contestants in a contest judged by a panel including actor and singer George Formby.

Morecambe Corporation, flushed with the success of the inaugural pageant, increased the first prize money to £100, and crowds of over 6,000 flocked to watch each of the weekly heats.

Lancaster's Jeanne Dunster was runner-up, with Marjorie Jones, from Wrexham, third.

June later became one of Britain's first pageant trainers, teaching aspiring beauty queens the secrets of poise and deportment on stage.

June Rivers,
National Bathing Beauty Contest winner 1946

1947

June Mitchell was seventeen when she won the 1947 National Bathing Beauty Contest.

Her success story began after she had won the 1945 Pin-Up Girl pageant and, the following year, Birmingham University Carnival Queen. But her beauty queen career ended abruptly when she quit the Miss Europe contest in 1949.

June was out in Italy representing England, but found herself overwhelmed by the unwanted and constant male attention. 'I have never been so frightened in my life,' she said, after booking a flight to return home to Birmingham.

Her father said, 'Human wolves surrounded the contestants wherever they went in Palermo, and even rattled on their bedroom doors.'

The prize money increased yet again this year to £500 for the winner, and an audience of 7,300 broke new records inside the Super Swimming Stadium.

June Mitchell is presented with the 1947 National Bathing Beauty Contest Rose Bowl by Sunday Dispatch editor Charles Eade

The runner-up spot went to Jane Morrison from Ross-shire, with Patricia Baines of Leicestershire, third.

Winner Pamela Bayliss (centre), Betty Spink (left - 2nd), and Marion Joyce Lewis (right - 3rd)

1948

There have only been two winners from Northern Ireland in the 75-year history of Miss Great Britain, the first of whom was Pamela Bayliss of Lisburn. She took the crown in 1948, two years after finishing runner-up in the Miss Ireland pageant.

A competitive athlete, Pamela got married in June 1949, delaying her honeymoon to allow for her latest race in Belfast.

The runner-up that year was Betty Spink from Halifax, whose daughter Gay would be crowned Miss Great Britain twenty-five years later.

Betty later recalled how very different her era of pageants was to that of her daughter's.

'It wasn't as glamorous as you may think,' she said. 'There was a lot of standing around in the cold and we all had to do our own hair and make-up. There was no interview round, either – we just walked round the pool and the judges would choose some girls to stay and some to go.

'But beauty contests were such fun back then; they were just light entertainment.'

1949

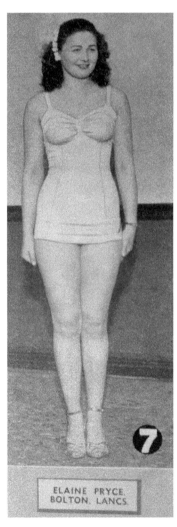

ELAINE PRYCE.
BOLTON. LANCS.

When Elaine Pryce, of Bolton, took the National Bathing Beauty Contest trophy in 1949, one newspaper described her as 'a beauty without the flattery of make-up', going on to rhapsodise about her 'smooth skin, graceful walk and natural manner'.

Elaine was a model, but told reporters she had two ambitions: to become an actress and to combine it with being happily married.

'A career is essential to keep a woman interesting,' she said.

Elaine carried on competing in beauty pageants and was later crowned Queen of Man during the Isle of Man bathing beauty contest.

Elaine Pryce the 1949 winner, from Bolton

1950

One of the biggest names in pageant-winning history was victorious in the National Bathing Beauty Contest 1950, securing the newly-increased prize money of £1,000.

Violet Pretty, from Birmingham, became an actress after her reign and was soon known to the world under her stage name, Anne Heywood.

She appeared in dozens of movies throughout her career, and was nominated for a Best Actress Golden Globe in 1967 for her role in *The Fox*, one of the first Hollywood films to portray a lesbian couple.

'I used the beauty business simply for the publicity,' she said, 'so that I could get a chance to go into films.'

Anne retired from acting in 1988 and now, at the age of eighty-eight, lives with her second husband in Beverly Hills, California.

Violet Pretty, the 1950 winner, soon to become actress
Anne Heywood

1951

Marlene Ann Dee, 1951 winner,
won the hearts of the judges.

Marlene Ann Dee holds the distinguished record of having competed in Miss World twice. While it is now a rule that contestants can only have the one shot at the global title, Marlene was able to take advantage of the fact that the Miss World pageant was brand new.

Created in 1951 by Eric Morley to commemorate the Festival of Britain, the very first Miss World pageant invited contestants from across the world without having to win any qualifying heat. Marlene Dee was one of many British contestants to take part.

After being crowned Miss Great Britain 1951 later that year, Morley decided to allow Marlene to compete in Miss World 1952 as well, where success again eluded her. She did, though, take the runner-up spot at Miss Europe 1953 – tying for second place with Miss France – after being crowned the very first Miss England.

Twenty-six contestants competed for the 1951 Miss Great Britain title, with Sylvia Wren of Dagenham second and Londoner Maureen O'Neill third. A crowd of 6,000 watched the event, judged by music hall stars Jimmy Jewell and Ben

Warriss, as well as *Sunday Dispatch* editor Charles Eade.

The top three were all firm friends from the beauty circuit; indeed, Marlene and Maureen had been guests at Sylvia's wedding a few months earlier.

The government of Australia had flown fresh sprays of orchids all the way over to Morecambe for the prize-winners.

But it was nineteen-year-old Marlene, from Henley on Thames, who won the hearts of the judges with her 'beautiful speaking voice, charming manner and lustrous hazel eyes,' and who attributed her beauty to 'plenty of fresh air.'

All the finalists received a £10 consolation prize and a week's holiday in Morecambe, courtesy of the corporation.

1952

Doreen Dawne had already finished third in Miss World in its inaugural year, but when she returned twelve months later representing Great Britain she failed to make the final five.

The 1952 National Bathing Beauty Contest was held in the pouring rain and high winds, yet every seat at the Super Swimming Stadium was sold out by 11am to watch Doreen beat thirty-five other finalists to the prize. Second place went to Sylvia Jenkins, with Brenda Mee third.

All thirty-six finalists had enjoyed a week's free stay at Morecambe Bay Holiday Park in the run-up to the pageant.

Judge Cesar Romero showed great class when asked if he preferred a winner to be a blonde, brunette or redhead.

'I don't like to generalise,' he said. 'Each girl is an individual and you cannot class them in bulk. The British style of beauty is universal, and I also think a woman looks more beautiful in an evening gown than in a swimsuit.'

Originally from Sunderland, Doreen changed her surname from Gaffney to Dawne, erased every trace of Geordie accent, and relocated to Chelsea where she became a singer and actress, counting Frank Sinatra and Bob Hope among her admirers.

But just six years after her big win at Morecambe, Doreen gave an exclusive interview to *The Sunday People* revealing she was broke, and had been obliged to sell all her beauty queen trophies to raise some money.

She was determined, though, to keep hold of the silver rose bowl she won in Morecambe. 'My big mistake,' she said, 'was not to invest the money I earned as Miss Great Britain into a dramatic arts course. Producers and directors won't look at you otherwise, and there are no short cuts, except for a few lucky girls.'

In 1964, Doreen narrowly avoided a prison sentence after being found guilty of attempting to defraud British European Airways with a forged exchange order. The Magistrates' court took into account her previous good character and let her off with a fine and a stern telling off.

Doreen managed to put her acting career back on the straight and narrow and in 1977 she was invited to celebrate her own Miss Great Britain silver jubilee by joining the judging panel of that year's contest.

Recalling her pageant days in an interview in *TV Times* to publicise the 1977 pageant, she said, 'The organisers were like army sergeants back then; you had to be at their beck and call. I told them, "Listen, nobody, but nobody speaks to me like that". The girls these days are prettier, too.

'Winning a contest was a hindrance, as there was a tradition that beauty queens weren't very bright. But beautiful people get better treatment than ugly people, and when I walk into a room I still feel the wives hating me.'

Doreen Dawne,
Miss Great Britain 1952 winner.

Doreen never married, but her death in 2005 catapulted her into the press again due to a battle between her brother and the Catholic Church over to whom she had left her estate.

1953

Brenda Mee, originally from Derby, was crowned the winner of the National Bathing Beauty Contest 1953, a year after finishing in third place. It was the second silver rose bowl to grace the mantelpiece of her basement flat in South Kensington – as her flatmate was none other than the 1951 winner, Marlene Dee.

Brenda was able to keep her winning figure despite her love for cheese, admitting to eating two pounds of Gruyere and Cheshire per week.

She went on to marry wealthy Australian businessman Ludvik Berger. Ten years later she divorced him on the grounds of cruelty, and successfully took him to court to force him to hand over shares in his businesses before he had time to dispose of his assets overseas.

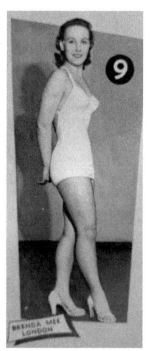

Brenda Mee, 1953 winner.

1954

It wasn't until 1954 that the title of the pageant was officially changed to become Miss Great Britain, replacing the rather less poetic National Bathing Beauty Contest.

Thus, Patricia Butler, a twenty-two-year-old model from Hoylake, was crowned the first Miss Great Britain proper, a year after having won Butlin's Holiday Princess of Great Britain. In fact Patricia was a prolific pageant winner, with twenty titles under her belt and prizes that included a television set and a refrigerator.

Runner up was Marilyn Davies of Stockport, and Patricia Bryne of London third, another former Butlin's Holiday Princess.

Films stars Glynis Johns and Anthony Steel judged, together with singer Guy Mitchell, impresario Jack Payne and *Sunday Dispatch* editor Charles Eade.

A crowd of 6,300 at the Super Swimming Stadium watched the contestants arrive by horse-drawn landau from the Morecambe Bay Holiday Camp, where the finalists resided for a week.

Patricia Butler, crowned the first Miss Great Britain in 1954.

When Patricia Butler again failed to place Great Britain on the winners' podium at the Miss World pageant, Eric Morley started to get restless at the lack of success on the international stage.

Above: Jennifer Chimes winning in 1955.

Right: Jennifer married comedian Max Wall in 1956

1955

Jennifer Chimes won the Miss Coventry title in, she says, 'a three-year-old swimsuit and with chipped nail varnish', after a neighbour persuaded her to enter just twenty minutes before the pageant was due to start.

Her prize was a week's holiday in Morecambe to compete for the Miss Great Britain 1955 title, but after the first night she packed her bags and went home to Leamington Spa. 'One night away from my kids, Martin and Julie, was enough for me,' she said.

Jennifer's mother persuaded her to return, taking the children with her. She did so, and became the first mother to win Miss Great Britain.

Tears rolled down her face as she was presented with the silver rose bowl. 'It's ridiculous,' she said. 'I didn't think it was possible for someone with two children to win the contest.'

Margaret Rowe, then the reigning Miss England and Miss Universe top fifteen finalist, took second place, while third was future winner Leila Williams.

Judges included singers Al Martino and Petula Clark, Al Read, Donald Gray and Ursula Bloom.

With grandma looking after the two little ones, Jennifer – married to insurance salesman Frank – travelled to London in a bid to become the first mother to win Miss World, in the days before the rules changed to allow only single, unencumbered women to compete.

She didn't win Miss World, but she cheerfully told the press afterwards that she was happy to be returning to her chosen career, that of wife and mother.

However, her words rang hollow just a few months later, when the biggest controversy to strike the Miss

Great Britain pageant so far hit the headlines.

Jennifer's romance with TV and stage actor and comedian Max Wall became public knowledge, and she was forced to speak to the press.

'Max Wall and I will be married as soon as my husband divorces me,' she told the *Daily Mirror* in May 1956. 'We are very much in love and very happy.'

Jennifer was by then living with Wall – famed for his 'funny walk' and unusual hairstyle – and the story caused a scandal. Not only was she 26 years his junior but both were still married at the time of the affair.

Furthermore, Wall had been a judge when Jennifer won Miss Great Britain, though she insisted, 'It wasn't love at the first sight'.

She was defiant in the face of public outrage. 'I'm not ashamed of what I'm doing,' she said. 'I think it is a bigger sin for two people to carry on living together when they're not happy, and I hadn't been happy with my husband for some time before I met Max.'

Wall himself, a father of five, had been divorced by his wife Marion just before he, with Jennifer and her two children, four-year-old Martin and eighteen-month-old Julie, moved into a rented flat in Brighton, but the public attention and disapproval brought the beauty queen to the edge of a nervous breakdown.

'She has been getting some very nasty letters,' the comedian told the press. 'I have sent her to a nursing home for a rest where she is safe from telephone calls and letters.'

This period of ill-health caused Jennifer to pull out from crowning her successor at the next Miss Great Britain pageant.

Jennifer's husband Frank divorced her weeks later, citing Wall as the co-respondent, but not before putting out a warning to husbands whose wives wanted to enter beauty pageants.

'They expose a girl to all kinds of temptations,' he said. 'As soon as Jennifer won that Miss Great Britain title I noticed a change in her. She kept saying she wanted to see her name in lights, and kept going down to London to have singing lessons with Max Wall.'

Jennifer married Max Wall in November 1956 at Brighton register office before making a home on the island of Jersey.

But after such an inauspicious start, life wasn't easy for the new Mr and Mrs Wall. Jennifer's son Martin was born with profound autism but, in an era in which disabilities received little empathy or understanding, she chose to care for him at home rather than send him away.

Daughter Julie, in years to come, recalled that 'she was an extraordinary mother. She refused to hide Martin away and found a way of teaching him by singing to him; she taught him some amazing things.'

Meanwhile, Max Wall's popularity was on the decline, not least of all due to the negative publicity surrounding his affair. He began drinking heavily and got into debt, and in 1957 collapsed on stage suffering a breakdown. He also, according to his stepdaughter Julie, subjected Jennifer to 'horrific domestic violence'.

Jennifer walked out on him in 1961, leaving a note that read, 'You will end up in one room, alone, with nothing.'

This prediction came true for Wall and he moved into a bedsit, bankrupt and estranged from his children. He divorced Jennifer for desertion and began a long, slow recovery, reviving his acting career with roles on stage and in popular soap operas and TV dramas.

In an interview with *The Sunday People* In 1967, Jennifer – by then working as a part-time barmaid back in Leamington Spa – said, 'The worst thing I ever did was agree to take part in that beauty contest.

'Looking back I can see the unhappiness it caused me, my family and the ones I loved.

'Twelve years ago I thought I was the luckiest girl in the world. I had a husband who loved me, two beautiful children – and I was the centre of attention.

'But success thrives on itself. I was surrounded by new friends, I couldn't move for reporters wanting to interview me. Everywhere I went people stopped to stare. I was living in a sort of dream world.'

Jennifer went on: 'I realise now that all the glamour and excitement was meaningless.'

She refused to go into detail about her two failed marriages. 'I don't want to talk about them except to say that I realise I caused a lot of hurt to a lot of people. But don't forget that I've been hurt, too.'

She admitted to finding contentment in obscurity. 'I've achieved a sort of peace now, and I love every moment of my job at the pub. I'm at last what I wanted to be: an ordinary mum.'

Max Wall told reporters that they stayed in touch. 'I'm still very much in love with her,' he said. 'I write to her and send her poetry, and if she's happy, I'm happy.'

The couple eventually divorced and Jennifer married lawyer David Coombes, her third and final husband with whom she lived until her death in 1994.

Max Wall died in 1990 from a skull fracture after falling in a London restaurant.

This unedifying episode caused Eric Morley to revise the rules surrounding married women entering his pageants.

He told the *Mirror*, 'I have come to the conclusion that married women should not be in this competition. Without being pious, when a married woman wins £1,000 and beats a lot of single girls, it is apt to turn her head.

'Don't start breaking up your home. Take your £1,000, go home and stay there and be happy with your husband.'

Sheila Forrest, later to finish runner up in Miss GB 1965, agreed with Eric Morley.

'There is a terrible temptation when you become successful to think you are someone special and different,' she said. 'You can become terribly unsettled and I know girls who lives have turned into misery when their engagements and marriages have broken up as a result.'

It was also the year when Morley caused offence to several celebrity judges when he called for a better calibre of judge in the Miss Great Britain heats.

'Red-nosed comedians don't necessarily have the experience or qualifications to judge a beauty contest,' he said. 'We must set a basis on which to judge and advise the judges what we're looking for.'

1956

Miss Great Britain 1956 was already a successful beauty queen when she took the title in Morecambe. But Iris Alice Kathleen Waller had won the Miss England title a few months earlier in very unusual circumstances.

The judges were unable to decide whether to award Iris the crown, or another contestant called Ilena Nelson. So, for the first and only time in the history of any major pageant, they called a tie, and both women shared the title of Miss England 1956.

The organisers decided to send Ilena to the Miss Europe contest, and Iris to Miss Universe, where she finished third runner-up.

Her victory at Miss Great Britain a few months later was unanimous, however, and put Iris in the running for the Miss World pageant. A severe flare-up of appendicitis meant she nearly missed the final, but she recovered just in time. Runner-up at Miss Great Britain was Walsall's Leila Williams, and third was Margaret Helsby of Ruislip.

The 6,000-strong crowd began slow hand clapping after being kept waiting an hour and a half for the judges – which included pop star Dickie Valentine – to make their decision.

Iris Waller Miss Great Britain 1956, advertising milk.

1957

Leila Williams – crowned Miss Great Britain 1957 at her third attempt - would become the last winner to go on to the Miss World contest; Eric Morley, frustrated at the lack of British success at his global pageant, made the decision to break ties with Morecambe Council and set up his own pageant.

This pageant, he said, would 'source contestants of a higher standard', who would do well internationally. Having been at the helm of the Miss World pageant for the past seven years, Morley felt able to gauge the sort of woman who could win the crown – and the Miss Great Britain winners didn't, in his opinion, fulfil that criteria.

Thus the Miss United Kingdom pageant was born in 1958. The fact that Morley chose to hold it in Morecambe's rival seaside resort of Blackpool, just forty miles down the Lancashire coast, only added to the competitive element which would, as we will see, become less cordial over time.

But back to Miss Great Britain 1957, and the crowning of another winner who would become a household name.

The papers reported that Walsall's Leila Williams 'broke down and sobbed' when the judges – including Bob Monkhouse, Tony Britten, and Joe Loss - reached their verdict after a nail-biting 95-minute deliberation, which was not, they said, unanimous.

The crowd - standing in a biting wind - grew so impatient for the results they began a slow hand clap.

In one of his recurring themes, Eric Morley said afterwards that the crowd's restlessness could have been avoided by having more professional, experienced judges.

'In my view this business of the judges getting their heads together to debate the results is wrong,' he said. 'Each judge should be independent, as they are at Miss World, and write down their individual scores. Those marks are added up by simple arithmetic and the highest scoring girls go through to the next round, and a majority vote decides on the winner.

'The result comes through fairly and much more quickly. The girls stood there today freezing, and the crowd was understandably impatient.'

That pageant also saw the last year of involvement from the *Sunday Dispatch* newspaper.

The Chairman of the Miss Great Britain organising committee, Ernest Kershaw, wrote in that year's souvenir programme that he, 'very much regrets the decision of the *Sunday Dispatch* to end this hitherto excellent partnership.'

June Dawson of Ellesmere Port was runner-up and Margaret Rowe – Miss England 1955 and Miss Universe finalist – third.

'I can't believe it,' Leila said afterwards, 'I thought I hadn't a hope.'

The 5ft 7ins drama school pupil said she would be putting her £1,000 prize money towards further acting tuition in the hope of becoming a success on stage and screen.

Part of her prize was a trip to Helsinki for a Fashion Revue, in the company of Miss Finland, Marita Lindahl – who, two months later, would be crowned Miss World 1957.

Leila struck an early victory for women's rights when she refused to wear a bathing suit when attending the civic reception held for her in her home town of Walsall to mark her Miss Great Britain win.

Leila Williams, winner in 1957.

The Mayor planned for her to appear in the same swimsuit she wore to win the crown at the Super Swimming Stadium, but Leila had other ideas.

'A bathing suit is a thing to wear on a beach or at a swimming pool,' she said. 'It is not suitable for a civic reception.'

In fact, it nearly didn't happen at all, when half of Walsall Council's hospitality committee expressed their opposition to a civic reception for Leila in the first place, with one former Mayor saying that such an event would, 'let down the dignity of the Mayor's office.'

She continued, 'If this sort of thing goes on, we shall be giving civic receptions to winners of the 'fattest lady' and 'knobbly knees' competitions.'

The former Mayor was overruled and Leila got her civic ceremony - but her bathing suit stayed firmly in the wardrobe.

Leila failed to make the final seven in Miss World that October, but her star quality was apparent and she was soon being lined up for acting roles.

When she returned to Morecambe a year later to crown her successor, Leila spoke in glowing terms about the opportunities the title had afforded her – though she admitted to finding being a beauty pageant judge herself somewhat hazardous.

'You make one friend and hundreds of enemies!' she laughed.

Leila's ambition to become a star was realised when, a year after her reign, she became at the age of twenty-one the first female presenter of the popular children's TV show *Blue Peter*. Sitting on the famous sofa beside Christopher Trace, she was the first of a long line of Miss Great Britain winners who would go on to become TV hostesses.

Leila was delighted that her TV career enabled her to stop modelling. 'I hate it because there is something so dead and inane about it,' she said. 'I feel an ass just standing showing off clothes, I want to do something real and active.'

She remained in the *Blue Peter* role for five years until she crossed swords with the programme's new producer, who fired her. The BBC's official explanation was that the show was being shortened by fifteen minutes and therefore only one, not two, presenters were needed.

Leila became an actress and appeared in several films and TV commercials, including a small role in *The Beauty Jungle*, a film shot in 1964 portraying the grim side of the beauty pageant world.

She met her husband Fred Mudd, of popular group *The Mudlarks*, on a BBC TV show, and they married in 1961. A daughter, Debra, soon followed and Leila retired from TV presenting to bring up her family.

Blue Peter fans were delighted when she returned to reunite with her colleagues for the programme's 20th and 40th anniversaries, as well as its 60th in 2018.

1958

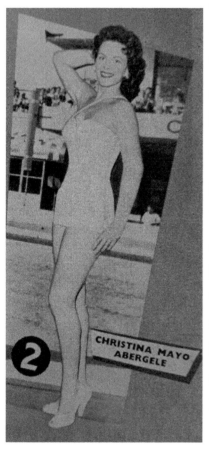

Christina Mayo, crowned first Welsh winner 1958

The absence of qualification into the Miss World pageant appeared not to affect the number of entries for Miss Great Britain, and the contest crowned its very first Welsh winner in 1958.

Christina Mayo, from Abergele, was another married winner. Soon after her victory she landed the role of hostess on TV's *Bid For Fame* quiz show.

Cricketer Johnny Wardle was a judge.

Like Leila before her, Christina also received a welcome home ball from the Abergele Community Association – but without the attendant protests.

Christina – real name Valerie Christina Weedman – found herself embroiled in a row with Mecca a few months earlier when she attempted to enter their Miss England contest. Eric Morley accused her – correctly – of being a Welsh national and therefore not eligible to compete. Despite Christina's protestations of dual nationality she was disqualified from the final.

Christina, who went on to have four children with husband Denis, died in 2018 in her beloved Wales.

1959

Boos mingled with cheers when Valerie Martin was named Miss Great Britain 1959, with many in the crowd expecting Marilyn Davies – the recently crowned Miss Blackpool – to take the silver rose bowl. But Marilyn failed to make the top three.

According to a reporter covering the event, Valerie's victory had come out of the blue, and she had never even been mentioned behind the scenes as a possible winner.

The lady herself was just as stunned, and even more so when the £1,000 cheque was blown from her hand by a strong gust of wind, landing in the swimming pool. Two students in the crowd promptly jumped in and rescued the very soggy prize.

Valerie had already netted £1,200 in prize money through winning pageants. 'It doesn't cost me a lot to enter,' she said, 'because my boyfriend drives me. I still have three finals to enter this summer.' (These were the days, of course, when all beauty pageants were completely free to enter, and all offered cash prizes to the winners.)

When told by a council official that under the terms of her new Miss Great Britain contract, she wouldn't be able to enter any more contests over the next year, she wrinkled her nose. 'Oh hell,' she said.

A movie production crew was at the Super Swimming Stadium that year, capturing scenes of the contest to include in the film version of the John Osbourne play, *The Entertainer*.

Valerie Martin, the surprise winner of 1959

As soon as Valerie had been named the winner, she was asked to act it out again, this time with Laurence Olivier as the master of ceremonies, and actress Shirley Anne Field playing the runner-up.

Thus Valerie became the only Miss Great Britain whose victory has become part of a movie – albeit one that she had to act out a second time.

Despite such a heady start to her reign and unlike most beauty queens at the time, Valerie had no ambitions to become an actress. 'Film work doesn't interest me,' she said.

Delyse Humphreys, of Sheffield, finished runner-up, while Dawn Read – who, at the age of twenty-four, called herself 'the grandma of the contest' – came third.

The judges included Al Read, Geraldo, Joe Loss, Bill Grundy, Chris Howland, McDonald Hobley, Mr P L Mead of sponsors Goya, with film star Tony Britten acting as scrutineer.

During the celebration dinner held for the contestants that night, Morecambe officials received 'furious and frantic' telephone calls from Eric Morley, demanding that the girls who would also be competing in his Miss United Kingdom contest should be over at Blackpool at his welcome dinner.

It was only the second year of Miss UK and the final had been arranged for the day after Miss Great Britain, in order to make travel easier for the eight girls who were competing in both.

But the gesture backfired when the eight contestants chose to stay in Morecambe.

Morley spoke to one of the contestants and asked her to get the girls into taxis bound for Blackpool within fifty minutes. She refused.

And Marilyn Davies, who had won Miss Blackpool a week earlier, was told that Blackpool's Director of Publicity was furious that she hadn't turned up and was considering putting a stop on her £250 winner's cheque for neglecting her 'duty to Blackpool.'

At the threat of having her prize money withdrawn, Marilyn took a taxi to Blackpool. None of the other girls went with her.

A Blackpool official told reporters that all the Miss United Kingdom finalists had been sent invitations to the dinner, which was also a chance to meet the judges. 'They all accepted the invitation,' she said. 'Having accepted it, it was very rude not to turn up.'

The obedient Marilyn Davies finished third in Miss United Kingdom; the seven who refused to attend the dinner failed to progress past the first round.

Morley wasn't happy. 'We shall introduce legislation next year to prevent the situation happening again; they either go to one, or the other,' he said. 'They certainly shall not go to both. It will be up to them to decide which is the more important to them.'

Valerie Martin made a ripple in the news again in 1963 when she was disqualified from driving after being found guilty of speeding – her fifth offence – and fined the princely sum of £10.

Valerie blamed her hectic modelling schedule. 'I know my driving record looks pretty grim,' she admitted after her latest court case, 'but the days just don't seem long enough. I am always rushing from one place to another all over the country.'

1960

Eileen Sheridan became the first beauty queen in history to 'do the double'.

She won not only the first Miss United Kingdom title in 1958, going on to finish sixth in Miss World, but returned to the pageant scene in 1960 to be crowned Miss Great Britain.

At the age of six months, Eileen was abandoned by her mother on the door-step of a seventy-one-year-old widow, Rose Clark, who went on to foster her.

'I shall use part of my beauty contest winnings to search for my sister Rosemary,' she said after winning Miss United Kingdom. 'I saw her two years ago with her foster parents but they both died and she went into a home. I also want to give my foster mother a holiday.'

Eileen, from Walton on Thames, proved a canny choice for both Eric Morley and for Morecambe Council, becoming one of the most enduring beauty queen names of her era.

As an Old Time Music Hall male impersonator, she was in demand for shows across the country, and Morley often invited her to provide the entertainment at annual events for Miss World contestants. Her drag act was, she said, rebellion against the permissiveness of the age. 'I'm fed up with seeing boobs all over the place on TV,' she said. 'I long for the romantic stories of the 1940s.'

Eileen Sheridan winner in 1960

Eileen gained notoriety due to her close friendship with the Krays, the heads of the much-feared East End underworld 'firm', testifying in court to vouch for Charlie Kray's character during his trial for the supply of drugs in 1997.

'It was a much nicer, safer place when the Krays were around,' Eileen told the jury. 'We could do with a few more of them around today.'

She also made news when she donated £5,000 to the British National Party (BNP) in 2009, one of only two major donors to the controversial far-right political movement.

Eileen's victory in Miss Great Britain was made all the sweeter by the fact that she beat the biggest beauty queen name ever to appear in the pageant. Rosemarie Frankland finished just third to Eileen, but a year later won both Miss Wales and Miss United Kingdom titles, before becoming Britain's first ever Miss World.

The author of this book was extremely privileged to meet Eileen in her home in June 2018.

Her cottage, on an exclusive estate in Weybridge, was almost hidden from view by an overgrown, jungle-like garden –

Rosemarie Frankland finishing third in 1960

deliberately so, she said, to keep unwanted visitors out. Her front window displayed warning signs of (non-existent) guard dogs, while inside the dark interior, all curtains remained closed.

Eileen was proud to show off her memorabilia from a life of showbiz. Every wall was adorned with photos of the Krays and various celebrities, while she pointed out various shotguns strategically placed in the hallway – 'just in case.'

The telephone rang, seconds after I had arrived. It was, she said, her minder, Jimmy Blue Eyes, to let her know that there had been a shooting nearby. I suspect that the real reason for his call was as a pre-planned check to make sure that this stranger who was visiting – me – was who she said she was, and not some villain from the past seeking revenge on a friend of the long-gone Krays.

Witty and frank about her beauty queen days, she recalled the occasion when Eric Morley had invited her to his hotel room in the mid-70s, an offer she declined. She was, in any case, completely devoted to her husband, Ken Price, a bookmaker whom she married in 1962 and who died in 2005.

'I was chatted up a lot by women when I dressed up as a man for my act,' she said, 'but I am definitely not a lesbian.'

She had brought all her beauty queen sashes out of storage for me to see, including that historical masterpiece – the first ever Miss United Kingdom sash from exactly sixty years ago.

Eileen was honest about her state of ill-health, warning me that she didn't expect to have long to live. It was still, though, a shock to hear that she had died just three months later, on 31st August. She was buried, as per her instructions, with all her beauty queen sashes, next to her beloved Ken.

The photo of the two of us together, taken by my husband that June day with her Miss UK sash, was the last picture ever taken of this legendary beauty queen.

Meeting Eileen Sheridan at her home in 2018

1961

In a sign of the shifting times for women, the Miss Great Britain crown in 1961 went to a university student for the first time. Libby Walker, a twenty-year-old from Blackpool, was studying at Nottingham University when she took the title.

A face that would become famous all over the world finished third that year. Lynne Shepherd, from Sheffield, evolved into comedian, actress and singer Marti Caine, winning TV's talent show *New Faces* and going on to land her own television series from 1979-1984. Marti sadly died from cancer in 1995 at the age of fifty.

Above: Libby Walker, Winner of Miss Great Britain. 1961

Left: Lynne Shepherd, who went on to become comedian, actress and singer, Marti Caine

1962

Joy Black became the first ever Scottish winner in 1962, but her victory as Miss Great Britain came just six months after a terrible personal tragedy.

Her two-year-old son, Macgregor, was accidentally shot dead on their 175-acre farm in Dumfries, and Joy had to be persuaded to carry on in beauty pageants by her husband Ian in order to distract her from her grief.

Winning the crown in August, 'took her mind off the great sorrow we have had,' Ian said after her victory.

Joy, twenty-four, told the press, 'When I heard that I had been picked as the winner I thought about my dear baby and felt like crying.'

Her win in Morecambe crowned a very successful beauty queen career, and she advised would-be contestants to just be themselves. 'Never take the contests seriously,' she said. 'If you do, you're finished. You will be unpopular with the other girls and that can be most unpleasant.

'Because I've done this for fun, I've made some wonderful friends, some of whom have come to stay on the farm.'

Her best beauty tips? 'Exercise, milk, green vegetables and plenty of fish!'

Another future Miss World competed in the 1962 pageant and, like Rosemarie Frankland two years earlier, failed to take the crown. In fact, Lesley Langley – competing under her birth name of Lesley Hill - didn't even make it past the first round in Morecambe. The Weymouth blonde returned to pageants undaunted in 1965 to be crowned Miss United Kingdom and Britain's third Miss World.

1962 was also the year that Morecambe & Heysham Council went to court to seek a temporary restraining order to stop Mecca ploughing ahead with its new title, Miss Britain. The council argued that it was so similar in name to its own Miss Great Britain pageant that the public – and even contestants – would confuse the two.

When the judge asked for a definition of a 'bathing beauty', the prosecution barrister replied, 'A young lady of British birth, aged between sixteen and twenty-six, who is agreeable to display her charms in a one-piece bathing costume.'

Amid laughter in the court, the barrister continued, 'It is very precisely stipulated that the costume must not include artificial aids or attachments.'

But despite several Miss Great Britain winners appearing in court to defend the council's title, Mr Justice Wilberforce ruled in Mecca's favour.

'One cannot easily monopolise a name of this kind,' he told the court. 'The word 'Miss' is used all over the world for beauty contest winners. And 'Great Britain' are words in general usage.

'There is no basis for a charge of deliberate piracy or confusion of the title by Mecca.'

Eric Morley was jubilant and joked to the press, 'I don't think the girls entering will get them confused.'

First ever Scottish winner, Joy Black, Miss Great Britain 1962

Ironically, it would be the press itself that would confuse the two, with examples of lazy journalism referring to 'Miss Great Britain' as 'Miss Britain' on several occasions in the future.

The first Miss Britain pageant was held the following month at the Lyceum Ballroom, London, and Suzanna Eaton beat twenty-nine other finalists to the title.

An advantage that the Miss Britain winner would enjoy over her Morecambe rival was automatic entry into the Miss International pageant in Japan, while Miss Great Britain led to no further contest once its affiliation with Miss World ended in 1957.

One consequence of this very public courtroom battle was an end to the friendly rivalry that had existed between Morecambe Council and Eric Morley, with far-reaching consequences for contestants in the years to come.

1963

The judges for the 1963 Miss Great Britain final included *Opportunity Knocks* host Hughie Green, singer David Whitfield and actor Jimmy Jewel.

Stockport's Gillian Taylor took the title, with Jackie White from Derby runner-up, and Cardiff's Hazel Williams third.

Morecambe Corporation called Gillian 'one of the most wonderful holders of the Miss Great Britain title, carrying out her year of service with dignity, grace and charm.'

As part of Gillian's prize she was flown to Dusseldorf to represent the country at British Week, an initiative that aimed to boost exports from Britain.

New sponsor Goya, the perfume house, also presented the winner with a statuette, in return for her presence on a tour of their head office in Amersham. Goya received priceless publicity as a result of their involvement in the contest and paved the way for other big-name sponsors over the next thirty years in the British pageant world.

Gillian Taylor, winner of 1963

1964

Carole Redhead of Poulton le Fylde was crowned Miss Great Britain 1964 in a year when the prizes significantly upped their game.

As well as the cheque for £1,000 and the silver rose bowl, Carole also won a £5,000 diamond watch and a trip to Australia.

Carole had had to enter no less than five heats in Morecambe before qualifying for the final, causing a *Sunday People* columnist to comment on the random nature of beauty contests, in which different judges make such different choices.

One would-be beauty queen, Anthea Wilson, was reported as having entered no less than ten heats that summer – and being unplaced in all of them.

Bob Battersby, Morecambe's Publicity and Entertainments Officer, could see nothing wrong in girls entering as many heats as they liked.

'With thirty heats, where would we get the girls from otherwise?' he said. 'We would be going down to the beach and getting the grandmothers to compete!'

Carole Redhead,
Miss Great Britain 1964

1965

Derbyshire's Diane Westbury was crowned Miss Great Britain 1965 following a beauty queen career that began in headline-busting controversy.

When she was announced the winner of Miss United Kingdom in Blackpool two years earlier, the celebrity judges disagreed very vocally about the result.

Singing stars Max Bygraves, Lonnie Donegan and David Whitfield protested that they had all chosen entirely different girls, before Eric Morley stepped in to explain the very complicated Majority Voting System he employed to find a winner in all his pageants.

In the scheme of things, Diane Westbury possessed a pageant pedigree that made her an obvious winner. In 1963 she won another Mecca contest, Miss Britain, which gave her entry into the Miss International pageant in Japan. She came second, the country's highest placing in the contest so far.

She also represented England in the Miss United Nations 1964 pageant, in which once again she found herself first runner-up.

At the time Diane was dating heavyweight boxer Johnny Prescott, a romance that cooled soon afterwards, much to the distress of the media.

Two years later she was crowned Miss Great Britain 1965 in Morecambe, having decided to revert to her original surname of Hickingbotham.

Ironically, one of the judges at the Morecambe final was none other than David Whitfield, who had protested so dramatically at Diane's Miss UK win two years earlier.

Diane Westbury, Miss Great Britain 1965

'I was alarmed when I saw that David was a judge,' Diane said afterwards, 'but it's turned out all right.'

And David was happy to confirm that, this time, he gave her his highest score.

Other judges included Morecambe & Wise, Hylda Baker and the first Miss Great Britain, Lydia Reid (now Johnson).

Diane remains the only woman in history to have been crowned Miss Britain, Miss United Kingdom and Miss Great Britain.

Runner-up to Diane was Southport's Carole Fletcher, with Sheila Forrest of Liverpool in third position.

With enough name changes to make the head spin, Diane returned yet again to the surname Westbury in order to launch an acting career, which saw her win minor roles in TV shows such as *Nearest and Dearest*, *My Brother's Keeper* and as a prison officer in *Crown Court*.

She married company director Malcolm Mendelsohn in 1967.

1966

The 1965 runner-up Carole Fletcher took the crown in 1966, and a year later she would hand over the title to the woman who came second to her: Jennifer Gurley.

To complete the synchronicity, last year's third placed contestant came third again: Sheila Forrest, of Liverpool. This is a sequence never repeated in any pageant in British history, but probably says more about the repeated attempts the contestants made rather than any more significant factor.

Carole, from Southport, was unemployed when she won Miss Great Britain 1966, having recently given up her position as a petrol pump attendant. She was therefore thrilled to land a new job as Miss Great Britain for a year.

The judges included actor Brian Rix and Eurovision singer Kenneth McKellar.

Carole Fletcher wins Miss Great Britain 1966

1967

Like Eileen Sheridan before her, Jennifer Gurley has the distinction of having beaten a future Miss World.

She won a heat of the Miss United Kingdom pageant in 1964, beating Ann Sidney into second place. However, Ann entered and won another heat the same year and in the Miss UK final, Ann took the crown – leaving Jennifer as runner-up.

Ann went on to win Miss World 1964 but, in a neat twist, was invited to perform the crowning ceremony of Miss England 1965 – won by Jennifer!

Jennifer, from Sale, Cheshire, represented England in the Miss Universe pageant before taking a break to establish her career as a canine beautician.

She returned in 1967 to the beauty circuit and finished runner-up to Miss United Kingdom once again, just two weeks before setting off to Morecambe for the Miss Great Britain final.

Jennifer Gurley, Miss Great Britain 1967

This time, it was Jennifer's glory, and her haul of prizes included a £2,000 cheque, the silver rose bowl, a two-week Mediterranean holiday and a flight tour of the UK.

The judges for the windswept, rain-soaked final included entertainers Jimmy Tarbuck and Dickie Henderson, and singer Kathy Kirby, all of whom huddled under umbrellas for the duration of the pageant.

1968

If any beauty queen had to sum up the spirit and fashion of the late 60s era, for me it would be Yvonne Ormes, Miss Great Britain 1968. At a time when the look was epitomised by long, straight hair, spidery eyelashes, pale pink lips, blue eyeshadow, thigh-high boots and short mini-skirts, this blonde beauty from Nantwich in Cheshire ticked all the style boxes of that period.

Yvonne Ormes, Miss Great Britain 1968

In my research into British pageants during this period, I was struck by the relatively small pool of contestants. The same names cropped up again and again, competing in one of the dozens, if not hundreds, of pageants that took place every year. Some of the girls that popped up regularly never seemed to win a big title, while others entered so many so often that it was only a matter of time before they won a crown.

Sheila Forrest, for example, finished in the top three on three separate occasions but never managed to capture the Miss Great Britain title. She did, though, win a nationwide search to find *A Girl in a Million*, a pageant run by ABC Cinemas attracting hundreds of entries, most of whom she had competed with at Morecambe.

But another of the most familiar faces on the circuit at that time – and one who really did win big – was Yvonne Ormes. A hairdresser's apprentice, she won the Miss Nantwich 1966 title at the age of sixteen, followed by a clutch of local titles in which she honed her craft.

By 1968 she was ready to step onto a bigger stage, and finished fourth in the final of Miss England, her first major pageant. This was followed by her first national title, Miss Variety Club of Great Britain 1968 and then, three months later, the big one, Miss Great Britain.

Entertainers Max Bygraves and Bernie Winters were among the judges who gave their top scores to Yvonne, with Sheila Forrest from Liverpool coming second, and Margaret Hudd of Dundee in third place.

After her crowning, Yvonne announced that she was quitting beauty contests to concentrate on her modelling career but, like so many girls before and after her, the lure of the glitter and glamour proved too hard to resist.

She returned two years later to win Miss England and Miss United Kingdom 1970, before finishing seventh in the Miss World contest.

Her last big win came in 1972, when she was crowned Miss Nightclub of Great Britain. This fifth major title gave Yvonne the distinction of winning more national titles than any other beauty queen in British pageant history, an achievement that remains unbeaten.

Yvonne also made history when she became the first woman to model not one, but two, Miss World crowns.

When winning the Miss UK title in 1970, she became the inaugural owner of a new crown designed specially for the pageant by jeweller David Morris. This stunning aquamarine and diamond sparkler became the official Miss World crown in 1979 and remains so to this day.

She also wore, for the first time, a rather less attractive crown, also designed by David Morris, during a dress rehearsal for Miss World 1970. This golden head-piece, reminiscent of a jester's hat, was 'accidentally' dropped and broken beyond repair a year later and never seen again.

Shortly after Yvonne's final pageant win in 1972 she married in secret, only telling her devastated parents a few days later. The union was not to last, but she found lasting happiness with second husband Alan Worthington, with whom she lives in Lancashire.

In 2020, Yvonne became the first British beauty queen to be immortalised on film, when the makers of *Misbehaviour*, based on the controversial 1970 Miss World pageant, cast actress Emily Tebbutt to play her character.

1969

Wendy Ann George's win in 1969 was notable for the fact that she beat a Miss World runner-up to the crown.

Kathleen Winstanley had become one of the best-known beauty queens of the era, finishing first runner-up in the 1968 Miss World pageant. She, like so many of her fellow Miss UK winners, took the risk of competing in Miss Great Britain the following year – only to suffer the ignominy of failing to make the top three.

The beauty contest world in the late 60s and early 70s was arguably at its most democratic. Winning a major title didn't give anyone a fair or unfair advantage; the best girl on the day won, regardless of past form.

So when Kathleen, from Wigan, took part in the Miss Great Britain pageant a year after finishing second in Miss World, and lost so spectacularly, nobody turned a hair.

In fact, Wendy George won the most hotly-contested pageant so far, beating no fewer than four previous or future Miss United Kingdom titleholders (Kathleen, Marilyn Ward, Jennifer Summers and Jenny McAdam).

Wendy Ann George,
Miss Great Britain 1969

After her reign, Wendy refused to step down from the pageant world, landing herself in the middle of an unseemly row a few years later, when she entered her name for the Belle of the Bar 1971 contest.

Having lived in her parents' pub – The White Swan in Derby – all her life, and regularly pulled pints behind the bar, she was perfectly entitled to enter the contest to find the country's prettiest barmaid.

But not all the other entrants were happy about having to compete next to a former Miss Great Britain. Said one contestant, 'I know it sounds bitchy, but it's a bit of a cheek for Wendy George to enter this contest,' while another agreed. 'It's not right,' she said, 'What chance do we stand now?'

The storm that had been brewing came to a head when, unsurprisingly, Wendy won the contest, plus a prize package including a glass-washing machine.

Runner-up Jill Madell was unable to contain her disdain. 'There was a lot of cattiness behind the scenes,' she told the *Mirror*. 'We didn't regard her as a real barmaid.'

Wendy herself was unperturbed by the backlash. 'Sour grapes!' she declared. 'I'm not a professional beauty queen, my full-time job is that of barmaid.'

However, the row prompted the organisers, the Society for Licensed Victuallers, to re-write the rules the following year, barring beauty queens and professional models from taking part.

In 1975 Wendy became the only Miss Great Britain to also win Miss British Isles, a rival pageant held by Great Yarmouth council.

In a pageant career of remarkable longevity, Wendy – competing under her married name of Turnbull – was crowned Southport's English Rose 1979, ten years after her Miss Great Britain win.

The two much younger girls who finished second and third to her – Tracy Dodds and Vivien Farnen – were both future winners of the Miss Great Britain title.

And Wendy also won back the Goya Perfume trophy she originally claimed as Miss Great Britain 1969, the scent company having transferred their sponsorship several years previously.

Wendy is still very much involved in the pageant world, having run several Miss Great Britain heats over the years and been a special guest at the contest's 70th anniversary final in Leicester in 2015. She also runs Beauties Reunited, an informal club which arranges get-togethers for winners and contestants from the 60s and 70s.

1970

The start of a new decade saw three notable firsts for the Miss Great Britain pageant: it was shown on TV for the first time, the final moved inside to a theatre, and the winner was the first to receive a crown.

The pageant finally burst onto the small screen in 1970, following negotiations between Morecambe Council and Yorkshire Television to screen the pageant to the entire independent television network.

Yorkshire TV chiefs needed to make changes to the show's format in order to produce a more entertaining watch for an audience at home, thus splitting the filming in Morecambe into three parts.

The swimwear parade took place at the Super Swimming Stadium as usual, a new daywear section at the Promenade Gardens, and finally the introduction of an evening-wear round, plus the crowning, at the Winter Gardens Theatre.

This format, which resulted in a one-hour broadcast, proved a success and was followed until the end of ITV's association with the pageant in 1980, except during the

Kathleen Winstanley, Miss Great Britain 1970

years of sponsorship by Pontins, when the winner would be crowned in its holiday camp ballroom.

Kathleen Winstanley's perseverance paid off in 1970 when she finally took the Miss Great Britain title. She was also the first winner to receive an actual crown, as opposed to just the sash and the silver rose bowl.

But her crowning provoked a storm of protest – and not, as may have been assumed, because a Miss World runner-up had taken the title.

The controversy arose when it was discovered that two of the contestants who had scored highly enough to put them into the final six were both eliminated in error in the previous round.

Chairman of the judges, Sir Norman Joseph, admitted the mistake, saying, 'Three of the five judges misunderstood the method of marking. We just assumed the scoring system would be the same as it was last year.'

But the judges – including Alan Whicker, Hylda Baker and Freddie Trueman – had been handed papers beforehand clearly stating that points awarded on the first day of the pageant would be added to those on the second day.

Some of the judges had assumed that the second day's scoring started afresh, leading to the confusion regarding the final points tally.

'It would not have affected the final result of Kathleen winning,' said Sir Joseph, 'but it may have affected fourth, fifth and sixth placings. It was our own fault.'

Several of the contestants demanded for the contest to be re-staged, with twenty-one of the twenty-eight finalists signing a petition. Morecambe Council promised to investigate, while confirming that although the marking system would remain, it would be explained to the judges more thoroughly in future.

One of the most vocal protesters was Birmingham's Maureen Pollock. 'We didn't want to disrupt things,' she told reporters, 'we just want to see fair play in the future. I don't harbour any ill-will towards the girls who were placed. It sounds like sour grapes on our part but that wasn't our motive. We only wanted to see a fair contest without this confusion.'

She added. 'This has been a miserable end to a smashing contest, because when I left everyone was on edge..

Journalist Anthea Linacre, a judge of several beauty pageants during that era, wrote a piece observing that some methods of scoring were so complicated that judges spent the evening trying to work out what was on their scorecard and not actually perusing the contestants on stage.

'For this reason,' she said, 'some televised pageants are judged during the final dress rehearsal and not during the live show, thus giving plenty of time to calculate the final scores.

'In other words, all the business of waiting for the judges to make their decisions is something of a hoax, since they made their minds up and submitted their final scores hours ago.'

As for the scoring itself, Anthea said that even the simplest of systems could confuse a judge.

'The mistake many new judges make is to mark the first contestant too high, leaving themselves very few higher scores for later contestants who may be more outstanding. The wisest policy is to mark the first girl six or seven out of ten, no matter how good she is. If nobody is better you can mark the others below five.

'I know of one man who delights in marking everyone the same, except for his favourite to whom he gives ten, ensuring that his winner is very apparent.

'I tend to find that women judges – in the minority on judging panels – have a greater sense of fairness than men. To a man, a sizeable bosom and long legs will make up for hunched shoulders, bad carriage and an over made-up face - all things which a woman will notice and mark down for.

'But as for the interview, both sexes will cringe equally at a precocious girl, one with a very marked regional accent, or those girls who are inarticulate and thick.'

That first televised Miss Great Britain pageant was hosted by Fred Dineage, but didn't receive much of a welcome from the critics. One bemoaned the fact that Miss United Kingdom, Miss Great Britain and Miss World were now all screened within a few months of each other, and were failing to hold the viewers' interest due to such similar formats.

'Perhaps a short clip of each contestant in their own home environment would be of more interest to the majority of viewers,' one reviewer suggested.

1971

When soccer legend George Best went missing from the Manchester United training ground, part of the blame fell at the feet of Miss Great Britain 1971.

Carolyn Moore, from Nantwich, Cheshire, was dating the sportsman at the time of his disappearance, and when he failed to turn up for training the press went wild in their assumption that he had eloped with her, with some even speculating that the couple were about to marry.

Carolyn Moore,
Miss Great Britain 1971

The twenty-year-old handled the barrage of almost-daily questioning from reporters very well, refusing to divulge what Best may have told her about his defection, and laughing off constant speculation about an impending wedding.

'I'm not getting married today!' she joked to reporters during one engagement, 'I'm working!'

The rumoured nuptials never took place and George went on to have highly publicised relationships with several more beauty queens, including Marjorie Wallace, Miss World 1973, and Mary Stavin, Miss World 1977.

During her on-stage interview during the 1971 contest, Carolyn told the host of her ambition to become a bank manageress.

'A woman bank manager!' exclaimed the host. 'I didn't know there was such a thing.'

The banks of London had to wait a little while for its next female bank manager though; after her romance with George Best, Carolyn became a Bunny Girl at the famous *Playboy Club*, where she was crowned London Bunny of the Year 1975, finishing runner-up in the international finals.

She refused, though, an offer to pose for *Playboy* magazine, saying, 'I'm not prepared to do nude work.'

In a little known or reported return to the pageant scene, Carolyn represented London in the 1975 Miss United Kingdom contest, but inexplicably failed to make the final fifteen.

In 2012 Carolyn was featured in a BBC documentary, *I Was Once a Beauty Queen*. It showed her, then aged sixty, living in a beautiful penthouse flat in London with husband Mark and reminiscing happily about her pageant days.

One of the most controversial contestants in the 1971 line-up was Dorset beauty queen Penny Mallett. She qualified for the final despite facing a charge of forgery.

After being interview by detectives at her local Bournemouth police station and being bailed for a month, she jumped into her car and headed straight to a Miss Great Britain heat in Morecambe.

Penny went on to become, under the name of Nina Carter, one of Britain's best-known glamour models, appearing as a regular Page 3 girl for *The Sun* newspaper, and as well as an actress and singer.

Finalist Penny Mallett became well-known glamour model
Nina Carter

1972

The Miss Great Britain pageant attracted its first major sponsor in 1972, when soap giant Lever Brothers struck a deal with Morecambe Corporation to promote its Lux Beauty Soap brand.

Elizabeth Robinson, from Nottingham, won the title and with it a cheque for £2,500, plus a diamante crown complete with a 'Lux' insignia.

Unusually for this pageant, this was the first time Elizabeth had competed, and she beat future Miss England Kathy Anders, from Rochdale, into second place, with third prize going to Wendy Redman, of Arundel.

Elizabeth Robinson
winner of Miss Great Britain 1972

1973

One of the most famous and enduring names in British pageant history took the title in 1973.

During the 1970s, the Spink twins – Gay and Zoe – dominated both the beauty business and the newspapers. The press couldn't get enough of these two beautiful, blonde and constantly cheerful identical twins from Halifax, whose own mother Betty had finished runner-up in Miss Great Britain 1948. They were always careful never to compete against each other, but between them they appeared in every major pageant, apart from Miss World and Miss Universe.

1973 was their stellar year. Zoe had been crowned as Mecca's Miss Britain and just months later, Gay won the Miss Great Britain title. The irony of twins winning pageants in bitter rivalry to each other was not lost on the press!

Four former winners were among the judges that year: Jennifer Gurley (1967), Gillian Taylor (1963), Christine Mayo (1958), and Brenda Mee (1953).

Both twins carried on winning: Gay took the prestigious Butlin's Holiday Princess of Great Britain title in 1976 and Zoe was

Gay Spink winner
Miss Great Britain 1973

crowned Miss Silver Jubilee 1977 by Sir Elton John.

Gay became a massage therapist and had three children with her husband Paul, whom she married in 1974. Paul gave his new wife his blessing to carry on competing in pageants, joking, 'As long as I get my breakfast!'

The only time Zoe competed in Miss Great Britain was the following year, 1974. She failed to make the top three, denying Gay the chance to pass the crown onto her sister.

The twins have remained in huge demand as mature models and have appeared on numerous TV shows, including the 2019 BBC series *Twinstitute*, which pitted sets of identical twins against each other to test various health theories.

1974

Marilyn Ward was considered a cut above her rivals in more ways than one when she was crowned Miss England and Miss United Kingdom 1971. A grammar school girl from Hampshire with nine 'O' levels, she was conversant in Russian and French and, despite stunning blonde looks, was a far cry from the 'bimbo' image that beauty contestants were accused of having at that time.

Marilyn went on to finish first runner-up in Miss World, but took the familiar gamble in 1974 by re-joining the pageant scene and entering Miss Great Britain. She admitted she had never been so nervous before a beauty contest, as she knew it was a risk she was taking after her success in Miss World.

'But I need the prize money to buy a house,' she said.

Marilyn's gamble paid off two-fold: she not only won Miss Great Britain, she ended up marrying her estate agent!

The new major sponsor that year was the National Dairy Council and their 'Milk for Beauty' slogan.

Each contestant received a copy of the Dairy Council's *New 7-Day Milk Diet*, despite none of them appearing to take more than a dress size 10.

Marilyn's start got off to a rocky start when she refused to sign the winner's contract. The *Daily Mirror* learned that she wasn't happy with the wording of the contract and that negotiations carried on between her and Morecambe Council for two hours immediately after the crowning.

'There was no question of a revolt,' Marilyn told reporters. 'I simply wouldn't sign it until some of the wording was changed. It was altered to my satisfaction.'

Geoffrey Thompson, Morecambe's publicity officer, confirmed that the problem had been a mere misunderstanding. 'I think Marilyn thought we expected her to work twenty-four hours a day on engagements for £10 a day,' he said. 'I assured her that that was not the case.'

Marilyn proved to be a very popular Miss Great Britain and capitalised on her high profile by landing TV hostess roles on Bruce Forsyth's *Generation Game* and *It's A Knockout*.

*Marilyn Ward, a Miss World runner-up,
crowned Miss Great Britain 1974*

1975

Despite a rumble of discontent over the results of the 1970 pageant, there had never been a full-scale uprising following the announcement of the winner … until 1975.

In the most controversial crowning in the history of Miss Great Britain so far, Susan Cuff was named the winner, only for some of the remaining contestants to storm off the stage during her crowning.

Their problem? It was all to do with that pesky Miss Britain title again, the one that had been the centre of the court case between Morecambe Council and Eric Morley in 1966.

Susan, a staunch Manchester City fan before it became fashionable to be so, finished second in Mecca's Miss United Kingdom pageant in the August of 1975. As an extra prize, Eric Morley offered Susan the title of Miss Britain and a trip to Japan for the Miss International contest.

(Mecca had stopped holding an actual live pageant to find a Miss Britain in 1973 and thereafter Morley offered the title to a beauty queen of his choosing.)

Susan Cuff, winner of the controversial Miss Great Britain 1975 title

By this time, however, Susan had already qualified for the Miss Great Britain final and, because she had set her heart on that title, politely declined Morley's offer. Morley was not best pleased at her snub and told her that she was no longer welcome to enter Mecca contests in future. He also threatened to withhold her

£1,000 prize for finishing runner-up in Miss UK.

The embroilment made all the newspapers and, as a result, by the time Susan went to the Miss Great Britain final she was far better-known than most of the other finalists.

In an extra Agatha Christie-type twist, an anonymous letter had been sent the day before the final to Geoffrey Thompson, Lancaster Council's publicity officer and chief overseer of the Miss Great Britain pageant, stating that the contest was fixed and that Susan was going to win.

When the written prophesy came true and Susan won the crown, it was seen in certain quarters as far too convenient. Susan, it was argued, must have known she was going to win Miss Great Britain in order to have turned down the other title.

It was all too much for many of the losing contestants, and they stormed off stage just as Susan was receiving her crown. In those days the pageant was pre-recorded before being transmitted on television later, forcing the producer to halt proceedings and have the crowning ceremony re-recorded minus the protest.

The rebel contestants had a straw poll amongst them, to choose the girls they felt should've been in the final - none of whom had made the actual final six.

The row went on through the reception and dinner after the pageant, until council officials relented – at the late hour of 1am – and agreed to unlock the safe and show the judging papers to the unelected 'shop steward', contestant Denise Brownlow.

The scoresheets proved that there had been no mistake; Susan had been the outright winner.

Contestant Yvonne Threlfell was still unconvinced. 'Even a week before the finals there was common talk among the girls that Susan was going to be the winner,' she told the *Sunday People*.

'We were amazed that she hadn't withdrawn. We just couldn't believe she'd throw up all the perks of that Mecca Miss Britain title just for the odd chance of winning at Morecambe.'

Yvonne conceded that she was certain the contest wasn't rigged – 'Not with the Bishop of Burnley especially on the panel' – but was sure that all the media coverage of Susan's row with Mecca had given her a subconscious advantage over her rivals.

'With that blaze of publicity, all the judges would be familiar with Susan's name and have her in their minds,' she said. 'Frankly, we couldn't see any way she could've beaten some of the other competitors if she'd started with the same chance.'

Runner-up Christine Owen, herself a former Mecca Miss Britain, and later to become a *Sale of the Century* quiz show hostess, disagreed. 'I know some of the other girls thought that Susan had stayed in the contest because she had inside information that she was a sure favourite,' she said. 'I think that's nonsense; Susan is a lovely girl who deserved to win. The girls who kicked up a stink and walked off need their bottoms spanked.'

Indeed, Christine was so upset by the commotion that she left the venue immediately afterwards and drove home, foregoing the reception and dinner.

John Fielden, a council official who acted as scrutineer for the pageant and totted up the judges' scores, delivered a deliciously withering put-down.

'The girls are just jealous. If some of them saw the marks they actually got, they'd be sick.'

The late, celebrated newspaper columnist and journalist Jean Rooke was among the judges that night, and wasted no time in launching into a tirade against the sore losers in her next *Daily Mail* column.

'I never actually believed those hoary old tales of beauty queens hating each other, with their aggressive, ambitious mums screaming 'Our Doreen should've won, disqualify the judge!'', she wrote, 'But now I know it's TRUE!

'I had never clapped eyes on nor read one word about the winner before she became Miss GB. About two-thirds of those girls, gifted only with good looks, gave a bad-tempered display of petty spite and enough narcissistic temperament to make Billy Bremner [a fiery Scottish footballer] look like a beginner.'

Susan herself was totally nonplussed at events. 'I've never even met the judges before,' she said. 'It's all so silly.'

Despite such an ignominious start to her reign, Susan went on to enjoy a high-profile career as hostess on the TV quiz show *Mr & Mrs* from 1977-1982, with her charming farewell catchphrase, 'Take care, lots of care.'

She has been married to top sports broadcaster and former Executive Director of The Football Association, David Davies, for nearly forty years, having met when they were both invited to judge the Miss Rochdale contest by local MP Cyril Smith.

1976

The 70s were the absolute heyday of British pageantry and a decade in which almost every winner of a major crown in this country went on to become a TV hostess. Miss Great Britain winners, runners-up and even losing finalists, popped up on television shows on a very regular basis: *Come Dancing, Sale of the Century, Mr & Mrs, 3-2-1, Play Your Cards Right, Gambit* – the opportunities were everywhere.

It was a bonanza era for making celebrities out of beauty queens and one that no longer exists. While quiz shows are still very popular, they no longer feature beautiful but passive women to lead contestants out on stage, or to drape themselves invitingly over the bonnet of that week's prize car. The role of women on television has moved on, taking with it the genuinely enticing opportunity of becoming a household name, a prospect no longer open to today's beauty queens, except those who may dabble their toes in the waters of reality TV shows.

Another winner who owes her success as an actress to her pageant career is Dinah May, who became Miss Great Britain on her third attempt in 1976.

Dinah, from Little Neston in the Wirral, married Bob May at the age of seventeen, but when she met comedian Bernie Winters, a judge at one of her first beauty pageants, it led to a romance that was to eventually end her marriage. Bernie stayed with his wife, but he and Dinah remained friends.

Aged twenty-four, she won the Miss Great Britain crown in Morecambe, having already appeared on minor TV shows, but her title led her to a far wider audience as a score girl on *It's An Knockout*, at the time one of the most popular programmes in the country.

She also became an actress, appearing in *Harry's Game* and *Blake's 7*, before landing the coveted role of

Dinah May wins Miss Great Britain 1976, with runners-up Gillian Clark and Susan Hempel

Samantha Davies in *Brookside,* a respected soap opera set in Liverpool. In 1984 she became the programme's first bride when she married on-screen fiancé Alan Partridge.

Part of her prize for winning Miss Great Britain was a holiday in Greece, and it was there she met local musician Takis, whom she married in 1977 after a whirlwind romance. The couple had two sons and divorced amicably in 2009.

In 1990, Dinah became film director Michael Winner's personal assistant, a role that she would hold until his death in 2013. Her memoirs, *Surviving Michael Winner,* provided an eye-opening insight into her life with him.

Dinah's runner up in Miss Great Britain 1976 also became a household name. Gillian Clark, a professional dancer, was chosen to join Legs & Co, the new dance troupe on the BBC's *Top of the Pops.*

Gillian appeared on the programme weekly for the next five years and the troupe gained pin-up status across the country. She last appeared on national television in 2003, when *Ant & Dec's Saturday Night Takeaway* brought the group together again as a surprise for a fan.

Pontin's Holidays made their debut in 1976 as the pageant's main sponsor, with the final held at their own Middleton Tower Holiday Centre.

Sir Fred Pontin and his spending power meant that the contest was able to extend the number of heats held across the country to sixty, necessitating the introduction of a semi-final to choose just twenty-one finalists to go forward to the grand final broadcast by Yorkshire Television.

Third place went to Susan Hempel from Blackpool – who would take the crown a year later – while one of the unplaced finalists, Madeleine Stringer, would go on to be crowned Miss United Kingdom 1977.

Susan Marcelle Hempel from Blackpool, winner in 1977

1977

In 1977 the maximum age limit to compete in Miss Great Britain was raised to thirty.

A council spokesman said, 'We believe girls are looking younger these days. So why should a girl who is lovely enough and has the right personality to win be barred?'

Despite this, it was a twenty-two-year-old who would win the contest held at Pontins Middleton Tower Holiday Camp - Susan Marcelle Hempel from Blackpool, who had come third the previous year.

One of her prizes was the year-long use of a car, emblazoned with the words 'Miss Great Britain' down the side.

Shortly after her win, the car was broken into. Susan's precious Miss Great Britain sash was stolen, together with £1,000 worth of clothes, bought specifically for a week-long nationwide tour, and all her Good Luck telegrams and cards.

'The car was a sitting target for thieves, belonging so obviously to Miss Great Britain,' Susan recalled. 'It was on day three of my tour and I was with a chaperone as I hadn't yet learned to drive. Everything was taken, and I was left with only what I was standing up in.

'I had a replacement sash made for me, but it just wasn't the same. About six months later I got a call to say my suitcase had been found. It was more or less empty, except for my Miss Great Britain sash.

'I was so happy to have it back.'

Susan's beloved mother passed away, at the tragically young age of forty-seven, towards the end of her reign as Miss Great Britain.

'I was so glad she saw me win the title,' said Susan. 'I think it kept her going. But I decided to put my replacement sash in the coffin with her so she could have it with her; she was so proud of me.'

Susan's nine-year-old sister Josette was her biggest fan, and during her crowning could be heard screaming her head off with joy from the audience. 'After our mum died I took her everywhere with me, and we're best friends to this day. Mind you,' she added with a laugh, 'she's the one who bosses me about now!'

The Miss Great Britain car appeared to be fated. 'I had just passed my test and was driving on the motorway with my dad as a passenger, on my way to open a new car showroom in Manchester, when I saw smoke billowing from the engine.

'I pulled over and we just got out and ran. Fortunately a lorry driver pulled over with a fire extinguisher and put it out!'

Despite such challenges, Susan has happy memories of her year as Miss Great Britain, and the friends she made as a result. 'We all looked forward to seeing each other in the next pageant, it was such a good time. And everyone was so natural: no Botox, no boob jobs.

'I really missed going after I'd won.'

As a measure of a winner's status in those days, the world-famous Hornsea Pottery invited Susan to their factory, where she signed her name on the bottom of a brown clay coffee pot. A few weeks later she was presented with a full set of crockery, each piece emblazed with, 'Susan Hempel – Miss Great Britain 1977'.

An entry form from that year states: 'Competitors are at liberty to emphasise their personality by way of make-up, head decoration and shoes. However, wigs and hairpieces shall not be worn. Bathing costumes MUST NOT CONTAIN ANY ARTIFICIAL AIDS.

'Costumes are subject to examination. Tights must not be worn with swimwear.'

The rules had also been updated to exclude any contestant who had previously competed in an international competition. This meant that the likes of Marilyn Ward and Yvonne Ormes – both previous Miss World contestants – wouldn't have been eligible had the regulations been in force a few years earlier.

1978

Patricia Morgan set no less than three separate records when she won Miss Great Britain 1978.

At the age of eighteen and three months, she was the youngest ever winner; as a South African national, she was the first overseas-born titleholder; and thirdly, up until that point she held the record for the longest reign.

One of the judges that night was Roddy Llewellyn, infamous at that time as a result of his relationship with the then-married Princess Margaret. He was pictured dancing with Patricia at the celebration ball afterwards, and admitted that he had found it 'difficult to pick a winner from so many pretty girls.'

Pat, for her part, didn't have her head turned by the Lothario. 'He is very charming,' she told the press, 'but far too old for me. I'm a John Travolta fan.'

Born in Durban, Pat moved to England at the age of twelve, and at first the Miss Great Britain organisers weren't certain if she was eligible, due to her only having lived in the country for six years.

'It was a last minute decision to let me take part,' Pat recalls. 'I think they nearly died when I won! They wanted me to say I was from Morecambe when speaking to the press, but I refused.'

Pat's only other pageant forays had been in the Miss England contest a few months earlier, where she made the top seven, and winning the Miss Tyne Tees Television title.

'Because I hadn't been around long I was seen as an outsider,' she said. 'But I was chuffed when I heard that the host for the night, singer Tony Monopoly, had put money on me beforehand to win!'

Patricia Morgan, Miss Great Britain 1978, with Princess Margaret's boyfriend Roddy Llewellyn

Pat proved to be a popular titleholder and the Miss Great Britain archive holds letters sent to the organisers praising them for their choice of winner, following events that she attended.

'There can be no doubt that you have an absolute winner in Patricia,' the managing director of Britain's top luxury car dealer HR Owen wrote to Lancaster City Council. 'Even at the age of eighteen she has the hallmarks of a personality flair that makes her so acceptable not only in the warmth of my family, but also at our function last weekend, where I estimate we had about one hundred millionaires present.

'The judging team are to be congratulated on the very fine choice of a charming young lady.'

Following Susan Hempel's dramas with the Miss Great Britain-branded car, it proved a thorn in the side for Pat, too.

'I was driving to an engagement not long after passing my test,' she said, 'when I saw the blue flashing lights of a police car behind me. I pulled over, thoroughly confused as I hadn't been speeding, and wound my window down. A policeman poked his head through and apologised for the inconvenience, but he'd spotted my car with Miss Great Britain down the side, and wondered if he could have my autograph!'

Other incidents while she was driving weren't quite as entertaining, including the would-be Romeos who would pull up next to her at traffic lights, winking and leering.

Worst of all were the drivers who would follow her up and down motorways for miles.

'It isn't so bad when I'm heading home,' said Pat. 'If I spot someone in the mirror trailing me I can just take to side roads I know well and throw them off. It's when I'm going to nightclubs for appearances that I worry about Romeos who see my parked car outside, then drift in to come and escort me out again.'

In 1984, Pat flew back to South Africa to visit family, and while there won a heat of the Miss South Africa pageant, putting her in the final. She chose to return to Britain instead, a decision she regrets. 'I wish I'd stayed to compete,' she told me recently. 'It would've been great to have won that title as well.'

Pat still lives in Whitley Bay with her husband Michael and is a keen golfer, having won many regional trophies over the years.

*With the postponement of the event in 1979 Patricia Morgan was
offered a six-month extension.*

1979

When ITV staff went on a ten-week strike over a pay dispute in August 1979, it was not only the longest and most costly walk-out in its history, it also had far reaching effects for the television shows in production. One of the programmes due to be broadcast during that period was Miss Great Britain 1979, scheduled for transmission on 26th September.

However, Pontins, the holiday camp company which had been the main sponsor of the pageant for the past two years, realised that holding the contest without a television audience would cost them an incalculable loss in terms of advertising and publicity.

They held an emergency meeting with Lancaster City Council to express their fears, and it was agreed to postpone the contest until the following spring 1980.

The twenty-four finalists who had qualified throughout 1979 were informed that they would have to wait another six months for their moment in the spotlight, while offering Patricia Morgan a six-month extension to her reign.

She accepted – despite the hazards of having to drive her Miss Great Britain car for longer – thus enjoying the longest reign in the contest's history up to that point.

Not all the contestants were happy to be given longer to prepare, though.

'A girl's looks can change a lot in six or seven months,' said one.

1980

When Miss Great Britain 1980 finally took place, the youngest winner was followed by the oldest, and the longest reign followed by the shortest.

And it was this latter point that landed Lancaster City Council back in court. This time, though, the plaintiff was rather shapelier than Eric Morley: it was the winner herself.

Twenty-eight-year-old Susan Berger was a statuesque blonde model from Hale Barns, Cheshire, who had been competing in pageants for ten years. She had been voted as having the best body on the circuit by her fellow contestants and was seen as a rival to be both feared and welcomed.

Miss Great Britain 1980 was Susan's ninth – yes, ninth – attempt to win the crown she so desperately wanted and, in a show of true determination, she won the title, live on ITV, with a panel of judges that included boxer Alan Minter.

So imagine her outrage when she was told that the title she had worked tirelessly towards for the best part of a decade was going to be taken off her after just eight months.

Main sponsors Pontins had made it known that they wanted the pageant to be held in January, at a time when viewers were most susceptible to their summer holiday advertising – and this meant culling Susan's reign, which would normally have ended in May.

Susan's fifty-two-year-old husband David was also her manager, and it was his decision to challenge the Council's decision, hiring the legendary George Carman QC – one of the best known barristers in the country, who had successfully defended politician Jeremy Thorpe just a year earlier – to fight their corner and seek an injunction.

Susan Berger, Miss Great Britain 1980, with runners-up Linda Lewis and Judith Hall

At the High Court, Susan explained to judge Mr Justice Whitford how important the title was to her. 'I fought for it, I planned for it,' she said. 'My whole image depended on it.'

Mr Carman stated that to lose the title prematurely would cause his client, 'financial loss, loss of status and personal distress.'

However, the judge was unconvinced that being Miss Great Britain for four more months would be of any real benefit, and refused – 'with some reluctance' – to grant an injunction to stop the pageant being held early, recommending that monetary damages should be paid to Susan instead.

Outside court, she was inconsolable, accusing the judge of having no understanding of the beauty queen business.

'It is not the money, but the loss of the title, that matters,' she told the waiting reporters. 'It is no consolation for the judge to say that I will always be Miss Great Britain 1980.

'How can I say I reigned for just eight months, when the other winners lasted a year?'

The 1981 pageant went ahead in January, as planned, but Susan wasn't there to crown her successor.

'I had been told that I could bring a chaperone of my choosing,' she explained, 'just as long as it wasn't my husband. If I can't take the man I love then good riddance to them.'

Another reason for David's apparent lack of popularity among pageant organisers was his objection to the contestants having to pay their own travel expenses to attend the contests. He aimed to start a 'union' to demand fairer conditions for the beauty queens.

Speaking to me recently, Susan said that David would be horrified to hear that contestants these days have to pay an entry fee to take part, on top of travel expenses and, in some cases, accommodation, due to the lack of generous sponsorship that the pageants attracted in the 70s and 80s.

The couple eventually retired to the south of France, where David died in the mid-90s. Susan remains in touch with many of the beauty queens of her era and I was delighted by her honesty and candour when speaking to her for this book.

Finalist Tracy Dodds made history that same year by appearing on both the BBC and ITV simultaneously. The brunette beauty from the Wirral was seen as a hostess on the BBC's popular *It's A Knockout* game show, while on the commercial channel she was competing in Miss Great Britain 1980.

1980 marked the final year of Yorkshire Television's involvement in the screening of the Miss Great Britain pageant. The BBC – having lost the rights to Miss World to rivals ITV – successfully bid to take over the broadcast.

1981

One proviso that the BBC made in bidding for the broadcasting rights of the Miss Great Britain pageant was that all contestants had to be a maximum age of twenty-five. This, despite current holder Susan Berger being twenty-eight.

Having been raised to thirty only a few years earlier, the new age limit didn't go down well with the contestants, with one pointing out that it was only when a woman hit her mid-twenties that she had acquired the poise and experience to carry the title off.

Another major change resulting from the BBC's coverage was in the pageant moving from Morecambe to London. Despite still being organised by Lancaster Council, and its qualifying heats remaining in Morecambe, television chiefs felt it made sense to bring the grand final to the capital.

That first BBC edition of the Miss Great Britain contest was held on 16th January in the West Centre Hotel (now the Ibis Earls Court), and hosted by actor Edward Woodward and radio presenter Ray Moore.

Woodward made it clear beforehand that he would be setting his own rules.

Michelle Hobson, winner in 1981

'I couldn't go in for any of those silly conversations about their ambitions to travel and meet people,' he said.

In fact, he didn't need to speak to the contestants at all; the interviews were conducted by a clairvoyant named Darlinda, who tailored the chat with the finalists according to their star signs.

The 1981 title was won by the 1978 runner-up, Michelle Hobson, of Kirkby-in-Ashfield, Nottinghamshire. She told reporters afterwards that the interview process 'felt like an audition for a job.' She added, 'All those questions from the judges were very unnerving!'

In shades of the Susan Cuff saga six years earlier, Michelle too had found herself embroiled in a war of words with Eric Morley and Mecca.

She had qualified for Miss England 1978 after winning the Miss Humberside title, but when the date was announced she found it clashed with another final she was competing in – the regional television pageant Miss ATV.

When Michelle chose to compete in Miss ATV over Miss England, Mecca accused her of breach of contract and slapped a life ban on her entering any of their future pageants.

Happily, Michelle went on to win the Miss ATV final, where qualification put her into the Miss Great Britain pageant. She came second to Patricia Morgan.

A year later, Julia Morley offered an olive branch of forgiveness to Michelle, inviting her to compete for Miss England again. Michelle gracefully accepted and entered the 1979 pageant, failing to make the final fifteen.

It didn't matter; Michelle went on to take the 1981 Miss Great Britain title. Linda Lewis, future *3-2-1* quiz show hostess, finished second for the second year running, while former Miss Scotland and Miss UK runner-up Marie Kirkwood came third.

At the time of her win, Michelle was engaged to garage owner John Littlewood. The relationship didn't last, and she went on to marry renowned Cardiff hairdresser Errol Willy.

In June 2019, Michelle's son contacted the Miss Great Britain office to inform them that his mum had died from cancer, at the tragically young age of fifty-nine.

He explained that because Michelle had been so humble about her beauty queen past, he was requesting a summary of the titles she had won so that he could include them in the eulogy for her funeral service.

I was able to supply him with a list of her many titles, plus some photos of his beautiful mum at the pinnacle of her fame, winning Miss Great Britain 1981, assuring him that, as a shining light of the beauty queen world during that era, she would never be forgotten by her many fans.

One contestant who found the 1981 contest more challenging than most was Caren Metcalfe, the first profoundly deaf finalist of any British beauty pageant.

Caren had contracted meningitis just before her fifth birthday and lost her hearing as a result, but refused to let her disability stop her from entering pageants. She was very successful, too, and her victory in the final of Miss Pontins gave her automatic entry into the Miss Great Britain contest.

She had to fight for her place, however. Just weeks before the 1981 final, representatives from sponsors Pontins and the BBC advised her to step down from the competition, saying it would be 'inadvisable' and potentially 'embarrassing' for her, if she were unable to cope with the live on-stage interview on the night.

Caren was understandably distraught, and it was only when a *Sunday Mirror* reporter took up her case and splashed it across the front pages of the paper that Lancaster City Council relented and allowed her to take up her place once again.

On the night, Caren didn't make the final twelve, but the most important battle had been won, not just for her, but as a landmark in the way disability was seen in mainstream life.

Vivienne Farnen took over the title of
Miss Great Britain 1982

1982

Regular finalist Tracy Dodds, from the Wirral, Merseyside, had to wait until 1982 to claim the crown, in a pageant held at London's Cunard Hotel and hosted by comedian Henry Kelly.

At the time of her win she was dating Andy McCluskey, of chart-topping group Orchestral Manoeuvres in the Dark, but pressure of work came between them and they split a few months later.

Her victory as Miss Great Britain crowned five years of competing on the circuit, in which time she won thirteen titles. Her pageant career would have started sooner, if the Miss New Brighton organisers hadn't found out that she was only fifteen and disqualified her. She won the title the following year.

Tracy was the third Miss New Brighton in five years who had gone on to win Miss Great Britain, following the successes of Dinah May and Sue Berger. (Three other Miss New Brightons had then won the rival Miss British Isles pageant, held by Great Yarmouth Council – Gillian Clark, Jeannie Lipton and Hazel Williams.)

It was a reign that began – and ended – mired in controversy over topless photos.

Shortly after Tracy had been crowned Miss Great Britain, topless photographs of her surfaced in a men's magazine. The organisers, mindful of the fact that they had been taken some years previously, chose not to sack her, while Tracy vowed to take legal action against the photographer who sold the shots.

Yet in November 1982 – ten months into her twelve-month reign – the twenty-one-year-old announced her resignation, by letter, to the organisers at Lancaster City Council. She wrote, 'My decision has been made for personal reasons. I would like to thank you for your help over the past sometimes difficult year.'

The council's publicity director Tom Flanagan said he would accept Tracy's resignation with regret, but admitted he was baffled. 'I have no idea what her personal reasons are,' he said.

He added that Tracy had made far less than the expected £20,000 earnings during her reign. 'We are disappointed for her, but the recession is the big problem.'

Tracy's boyfriend at the time told the press: 'Tracy has quit. There is no point denying it, but the reasons are her own affair. The last few weeks have been anything but easy for her and finally she had to make the decision to resign for the sake of her own career.'

The runner-up in the 1982 pageant, Vivienne Farnen, was hastily anointed as the new Miss Great Britain for the last two months of her reign.

Tracy Dodds, who resigned as Miss Great Britain 1982

The reason for Tracy's shock decision was soon revealed, when vodka makers Vladivar unveiled their new calendar, featuring the topless beauty queen as one of their models.

The Miss Great Britain contract forbids topless or nude work, and with the calendar due to be launched more than a month before the end of her reign, she had no choice but to resign.

'I resigned for the sake of my career,' Tracy told the press. 'People think if you win Miss Great Britain you're made for life, but it's just not the case.'

Thirty years later, Tracy was featured in a BBC documentary *I Was Once a Beauty Queen,* which re-visited several past winners. Viewers learned that, having married and settled in Australia, Tracy's husband left her for a younger woman.

She returned to Merseyside, studied for a First Class degree and became a teacher, eventually quitting the profession and marrying for a second time.

1983

Rose McGrory became only the second winner from Northern Ireland when she took the Miss Great Britain crown in 1983 in the Palm Lounge of London's Waldorf Hotel.

The twenty-five-year-old had won the Miss Northern Ireland title in 1978 under her maiden name of Davey, and after competing in the Miss United Kingdom pageant had declared that she was retiring from the beauty circuit.

But two years after marrying motor mechanic David McGrory, she decided to give it one last shot – and ended up as Miss Great Britain.

Rose's employer, Ulster Bank in Belfast, had more reason to cheer than many, as her colleague, Alison Smyth, had finished runner-up to Miss United Kingdom a few months beforehand.

In fact, both Rose and Alison had also competed together in the 1981 Miss Great Britain heats but, while Rose made it through to the final on that occasion, her co-worker had missed out.

Rose McGrory, Miss Great Britain 1983, with runners-up Victoria Ellis and Karen Moore

An Ulster Bank spokesman said they were thrilled about Rose's win, adding, 'She is a typical Irish beauty with lovely colouring and big brown eyes. She is also a very nice, very modest girl.'

In the September of her reign, she narrowly escaped injury when her car was attacked as she drove through Dublin. As she slowed at traffic lights a man smashed the front passenger seat window with an iron bar and grabbed her handbag. 'I got a dreadful fright,' she said. 'I thought it was a bomb smashing against the window.'

Victoria Ellis from Ellesmere Port was runner-up to Rose, while Southsea's Karen Moore – who later that year went on to become Miss England and place fourth runner-up at Miss Universe – finished third.

1984

In a true sign of success, Debbie Greenwood is better known for her television presenting work than for being a former beauty queen.

The Liverpool brunette had only been married to husband Philip Eccles for five months when she was crowned Miss Great Britain 1984.

And just four weeks after her crowning, she landed a role as presenter at Granada TV. Her on-screen skills so impressed executives at the BBC that she was headhunted to present their flagship *Breakfast Time* programme – but not before Granada threatened the BBC with an injunction, later dropped, claiming that Debbie had broken her contract with them.

Debbie replaced Selina Scott on *Breakfast Time,* and her co-host Frank Bough, with characteristic bluntness, admitted to a few teething troubles. 'Selina is very experienced, and Debbie is not,' he said after her first show. 'She has a lot of professional habits to learn, but she is very Liverpool, which is a terrific asset.'

Her high profile and beauty queen past left her open to criticism from newspaper columnists and reviewers. 'It used to really hurt me,' she said. 'Often the knocks weren't even about my ability to do the job, they were on a personal level, like the clothes I wore.

Debbie Greenwood, Miss Great Britain 1984 (L) with successor Jill Saxby

Most of the popular rags have taken the line that because I'm an ex-beauty queen you can't expect much from me in the brains stakes. It's funny – nobody equates ugliness with intelligence, but beauty equals no brains.'

Debbie's marriage to her first husband ended in divorce and in 1988 she met Scottish television presenter Paul Coia, whom she married in 1992 and with whom she has two daughters.

She went on to present on shopping channel QVC for twelve years and was co-founder of The Craft Channel. She now runs a consultancy specialising in the coaching of shopping channel presenters.

Runners-up in the 1984 Miss Great Britain pageant were Belfast's Amanda Henry, and Diana Brookes from Liverpool.

1985

Jill Saxby from Sheffield carries the distinction of being the winner of the last beauty contest ever shown on BBC television.

After her triumph in 1985, Michael Grade, at that time the BBC Controller of Programmes, axed Miss Great Britain from the screens – calling it 'an anachronism in this day and age of equality, and verging on the offensive'.

The Sun newspaper vehemently disagreed. 'Rubbish!' said an editorial piece. 'They're still a whole lot of fun and still hold a fascination for men – and women. This may be difficult for the bores at the BBC to understand, but the fact that they top the ratings every year shows it is true.'

Despite the might of Britain's best-selling newspaper getting behind them, beauty pageants never made a return to BBC screens, and comedian Tom O'Connor hosted the last ever show from London's Waldorf Hotel.

Winner Jill Saxby married snooker legend Willie Thorne, her second husband, after they met at the World Snooker Championships in Sheffield in 1994.

Thorne had never hidden his love for gambling but, following his retirement from snooker in 2002, his addiction careered out of control.

In 2015, Jill told the press of their desperate situation. A year earlier she had found her husband sobbing uncontrollably in a hotel room after gambling debts of £1m had left him severely depressed.

In fact, the snooker star had booked into a hotel planning to take his own life, such was his despair about the debts racked up by a gambling addiction that, at its worst, saw him place up to £20,000 on a single race.

Jill and Willie Thorne appeared on ITV's *This Morning* breakfast show that same month, where Jill described finding Willie in such a state as 'heartbreaking'.

'I knew I'd only just caught him in time,' she said. 'He was hellbent on doing it. Depression is like watching someone die,' she added.

Thorne explained on the programme that he had declared himself bankrupt, and that the couple had cleared their home of all possessions – including his sporting trophies – to prevent them being seized by bailiffs.

Just a month later, in June 2015, Thorne revealed he was suffering from prostate cancer. He credits Jill as his rock. 'Without her love and support, I don't know what I would've done,' he said. 'She is so incredibly understanding and when I needed someone to lean on, she was there. She has the heart of a lion.'

The couple split up in November 2019, the strain of their precarious financial situation being too much to bear. Sadly, Willie died in hospital in Spain in June 2020 from leukaemia. Jill said, 'I was with him via video link at the end. We loved each other so much.'

Jill Saxby crowned Miss Great Britain 1985, with runners-up Susan Cooper and Lesley-Ann Musgrave

1986

Lesley-Ann Musgrave, from Hartlepool, became the first Miss Great Britain to miss out on a televised crowning as a result of the BBC's decision, one that incensed Lancaster Council's Director of Publicity and Amenities Tom Flanagan.

'We had a marvellous line-up of girls, the best I've known in the nine years I've been associated with the competition,' he told *The Stage*.

'I regret it went untelevised because those finalists deserved that level of national media exposure.'

He was also angry that the town of Morecambe was missing its usual publicity boost from having a televised final and the resultant news coverage.

Mr Flanagan laid the blame for the TV ban firmly at the door of Michael Grade. 'Without his personal intervention, I am convinced that the usual eight to twelve million would've watched the 1986 final', he said. 'We are still well within the currency of our contractual term with the BBC.

Lesley-Ann Musgrave, Miss Great Britain 1986

'The existing agreement calls for coverage of the 1986 and 1987 events. That's what everyone finds particularly annoying. If the BBC had wished to drop Miss Great Britain when the question of contract renewal arose, we would've accepted their right to do so without resentment.'

On the upside, Mr Flanagan said that Miss Great Britain was 'easier to present without the restraints and requirements of a television production team interfering with the timing and continuity of the actual stage show.'

He also saw the break as a chance to rethink the format of the pageant for a modern-day audience.

'What bores the critics is the total predictability of each programme, from the embarrassment of those unreal interviews, to the inevitable announcements in reverse order.'

'We are keen on new themes and innovations. For example, our in-depth interviews take place behind closed doors, but these exchanges between the contestants and the judging panel would make a fascinating, fly on the wall documentary.'

Indeed, it is the interview section, he said, that weeded out those least capable of carrying out an ambassadorial role as Miss Great Britain.

'For the same reason,' he continued, 'we resist the temptation to earn income from fashion trade sponsorship where a firm kits out each girl in a given vein. Instead our competitors pick their own swimwear, daywear and evening gowns and we discuss their choices quite intricately in interview. After all, Miss Great Britain must be able to choose the best outfit from her own wardrobe for each of her diverse engagements, ranging from opening motor showrooms to being present at royal functions.'

He didn't expect Michael Grade's TV ban to impact on bookings for the new winner, Lesley-Ann Musgrave, though. 'The title itself has such a special degree of reputation and credibility that I doubt she will undertake a lighter workload than her predecessors.'

Mr Flanagan was keen to emphasise exactly how much publicity Morecambe gained through the pageant.

'It's not just the opening scene-setting shots of the town or the odd mention throughout the show,' he said. 'It's a year-round PR exercise, with the heats of the contest running for fourteen weeks in Morecambe, playing a major part of the resort's entertainment programme for the summer season.'

This sustained local coverage was in stark contrast to that of the national press, who would generally concentrate their interest in the few days before the final, concluding after they'd got their photo of the winner in bed with a glass of champagne in hand, crown on head.

'So really,' Mr Flanagan concluded, 'it's only the BBC audience who have been deprived by Michael Grade's decision, not the town of Morecambe. We will continue to attract competitors and in fact this year we saw a lot of newcomers, completely fresh to the beauty scene, which indicates a growing interest in the contest – ironically, in the year the BBC turned its back on us.'

And he had only encouraging words for Lesley-Ann, Morecambe's first unseen queen. 'Her modelling career is now worth at least three times what it was before last week's final.'

TV presenter Debbie Greenwood, the 1984 winner who attended that year's pageant, agreed. 'You make valuable contacts. To go through your reign and end up on the dole, you'd have to be utterly hopeless.'

Debbie had predicted a year earlier that the 1985 contest would be the last shown on the BBC.

'Michael Grade is acting like an extreme feminist when there are far more vital feminist issues to be dealing with.' she said.

1987

Winning twenty-five beauty titles by the age of twenty is an impressive enough statistic, but for Linzi Butler, from Southport, it was a pageant career that began early.

At the age of four, she won the celebrated Miss Pears crown. The contest, which ran from 1958 to 1997, was organised by the soap manufacturer to select a young brand ambassador.

Linzi was clearly following in family footsteps: her mum Margaret had won numerous titles and was crowned Miss Yorkshire 1972 in the same year that her young daughter was crowned Miss Pears!

At sixteen, she became the youngest-ever winner of the Miss Blackpool pageant in 1982. The title qualified her for the Miss United Kingdom contest but, with the minimum age limit being seventeen, she was too young, and had to wait until 1985 when she qualified for the big final again.

Linzi was the only Miss Great Britain to have previously won an American national beauty title, having scooped the Miss Legs of America crown while working for her family's US-based antiques business.

As well as a cheque for £4,000, one of Linzi's prizes was two guest spots on the ITV quiz show *Sale of the Century*. Host Derek Batey, who compered the final of the pageant, said, 'One or two of the questions on the show are visual, and this is where Miss Great Britain will come in. She will model the earrings, raincoat, etc, and assist our regular hostess.

'Border TV has a long relationship with the Miss Great Britain contest, starting with one of our original hostesses, Susan Cuff, Miss Great Britain 1975.'

Linzi's boyfriend at the time of her Miss Great Britain win was Gary Bell, whose sister Gillian took the crown from Linzi one year later in 1988. When Gary married Linzi a year later, he was in the unique position of having a former Miss Great Britain in both a wife and a sister!

The runner-up prize went to Susan Cooper, from Hull, with Sheffield's Zoe Bolsover in third.

The Butler family completed a remarkable triple in 1993, when Linzi's younger sister Melanie also competed in Miss United Kingdom, making it the family's third appearance in this pageant, following Linzi in 1985 and mum Margaret back in 1968.

Linzi Butler, Miss Great Britain 1987, with Mr & Mrs hosts Derek Batey and Donna Mayers

1988

Unbeknown to Lancaster Council at the time, the 1988 pageant would be the penultimate under their ownership – and it got off to a rocky start due to a series of malicious phone calls. Council officials, as well as several local newspaper reporters, were subjected to anonymous calls from a woman, claiming that one of the finalists in the pageant had had an abortion leading to her being disqualified.

Tom Flanagan, Director of Publicity & Amenities at the council, hit out at the accusations. 'I am appalled by these malicious calls,' he said. 'I want to stress that nobody has been disqualified. The caller claims to be a member of an anti-abortion organisation and said that we should know that one of the five Merseyside finalists had had an abortion. But whether a contestant has had an abortion or not is of no concern of ours.'

The pageant was held at Birmingham's National Exhibition Centre as part of its four-day *Holiday and Travel Fair* and proceeded without any further hitches.

Gillian Bell, of Liverpool, was crowned Miss Great Britain 1988 by her predecessor Linzi Butler, her future sister-in-law.

Merseyside pulled off a hat-trick this year, with the runners-up, Justine Ealey and Victoria Ellis, also hailing from the area.

The writing appeared to be on the wall for Morecambe's investment in the Miss Great Britain pageant, when only two contestants turned up for one of the heats that summer. Both girls shared the cash prize.

With the magnificent Super Swimming Stadium long since demolished in 1975, all Morecambe heats had been moved inside to the Superdome complex and staged as part of the evening entertainment programme.

Morecambe's Labour councillors had already started to campaign for the town to end the competition once and for all, but their Tory rivals argued that the pageant still provided the best publicity possible, with the new format at the National Exhibition Centre giving it a fresh boost.

In a meeting held in March 1988, the council narrowly agreed by thirty votes to continue holding the pageant for the next two years.

Gillian Bell Miss Great Britain 1988, with runners-up
Victoria Ellis and Justine Ealey and judge Mark 'Rollerball' Rocco

Left: Amanda Dyson, winner in 1989 of the final edition under the current owner

Below: The last Official Programme under the ownership of Lancaster Council

THE
MISS GREAT BRITAIN
1989
GRAND FINAL

Presented by
MORCAMBE TOURISM

in association with
HOLIDAY CLUB PONTIN'S

Sunday, 8th January 1989
at 2.00pm

Compere:
DEREK BATEY
with
KEITH MONK AND HIS MUSIC
plus
STAR CABARET

OFFICIAL PROGRAMME

1989

Despite Lancaster Council voting to keep the pageant for two more years, 1989 would prove to be the final edition under its ownership.

Pontin's held heats throughout the summer at its holiday parks, with a semi-final taking place in its Weston-Super-Mare village.

The grand final, in January 1989, returned to Birmingham's NEC with Derek Batey as compere once more, and was won by Amanda Dyson from Barrow in Furness, who intrigued the judges with her job as a lathe operator for a shipbuilder.

But in August 1989, the die was cast, and Lancaster Council put the Miss Great Britain pageant up for sale.

In an interview with *The Guardian*, Tom Flanagan, Director of Publicity & Amenities, explained the council's reluctant decision. 'At first, the move away from the event was mostly on political lines, with the Conservatives strongly in favour of keeping it. But even their support fell away when they saw that nobody was coming to the contest anymore, and it was then put up for tender.'

Eileen Blamire, the Labour chair of the council's arts and events committee at that time, was determined that they would never stage the pageant again.

'We were all so naïve in our twenties and thirties,' she said. 'But when women started going on to platforms to protest, I started thinking. Those women changed ideas. We woke up and asked ourselves what we were doing, spending time watching women being paraded like this? And then it seemed bygone, outdated and boring. It didn't take a revolution; it was dead and the audiences were gone.'

One person who was quick to put in a bid for the franchise was Liverpool businesswoman Joy Freeman.

As Joy Black she had won the Miss Great Britain 1962 pageant, before starting up her own successful modelling agency and offering catwalk training to budding beauty queens.

She declined to say how much she had offered for the iconic competition, which included TV rights and preliminary heats, but revealed she was up against one other bidder, 'a local multi-millionaire'.

'I believe I have a good chance of winning it, with my experience. And I know what goes on behind the scenes,' she said.

Sadly for Joy, the local multi-millionaire was the successful bidder. Impresario Harvey Pritchard was no stranger to beauty pageants; his sister was none other than Julia Morley, CEO of the Miss World organisation and wife of Eric.

The irony of the Miss Great Britain pageant turning full circle and returning to the Morley family, forty-five years after that first contest held by a windswept swimming pool, was not lost on Pritchard, who vowed to relaunch the contest in an exciting new format in July 1990.

This gave reigning queen Amanda Dyson an extended term of office. But nobody could envisage at the time that this new pageant would never happen, and that Amanda would end up being Miss Great Britain for three years, easily eclipsing the record set by Pat Morgan when the 1979 contest was cancelled.

'I knew I was going to be the last Miss Great Britain in this current format,' she told *The Guardian*, 'because the council was trying to sell it even then.'

Pritchard bought the title mid-way through Amanda's reign, and the union proved to be an unhappy one for both her and the council.

'I did one job for him,' she said, 'opening a hotel gym in Lancaster. He then took me to see an agent in London as he wanted to get the pageant back on television. But the only thing that came out of that was a nasty spread about me in *The Sunday Sport* newspaper.'

Repeated attempts to contact Pritchard by both her and the council failed. The council was told that the £48,000 sale of the pageant to him had failed, and the money never materialised, forcing them to seek legal action to try to recover their losses.

'I'd like to pass the title on in some way,' Amanda said, 'and get back to being myself again.'

1993 - 1995

After the Pritchard debacle, Lancaster Council put the Miss Great Britain contest back on the market, to be snapped up for a bargain £10,000 by Pontins – the holiday camp company that had been so instrumental in sponsoring the pageant back in the 70s.

Pontins' managing director Graham Parr vowed to give the contest a revamp and get it back on television.

'There is no doubt that the TV people have decided beauty contests are dead and buried,' he said, 'but we think there is mileage in a new format, a broader-based competition that's not just about face and figure.'

In the event, Pontins didn't ever get to stage a Miss Great Britain pageant and the title lay unused and unloved for the next four years.

(Left to right), Kathryn Middleton (1993); Michaela Pyke (1994); and Sarah-Jane Southwick (1995)

A search online of Miss Great Britain winners from 1993-1995 names Kathryn Middleton, Michaela Pyke and Sarah-Jane Southwick as the official titleholders, but this information is disputed. All three won the Miss British Isles title and represented Great Britain in Miss Universe, but none of them were officially winners of a Miss Great Britain pageant.

I often refer to the 1990s as the 'dark days' of pageantry, an era in which beauty contests either fell by the wayside due to their perception as being outdated and politically incorrect, or were completely ignored by the press and media.

It would be some years before mass use of the internet would bring the popularity of pageants back to life via a vast online audience, and as a result I have found my research into winners and contestants from this decade to be extremely challenging due to lack of available resources and information.

1996

No Miss Great Britain pageant took place in 1995 in any shape or form, but a year later saw yet another new start for a title that had been rapidly losing its identity.

Businessman John Singh, owner of Worldwide Snooker Promotions, began his pageant involvement by offering sponsorship to the Miss United Kingdom contest in 1994.

His appetite for pageants duly whetted, he was canny enough to discover that the Miss Great Britain trademark was up for grabs, having been left to languish, unwanted and unloved, after Pontins' abortive attempt to revive the brand several years earlier.

Anita St Rose, the first black winner of Miss Great Britain in 1996

Singh snapped it up, a move which would allow him in future to offer the franchise to run Miss Great Britain to individuals and businesses at considerable profit to himself.

But in 1996, he wanted to run it himself. His first winner made history as the first – and to date only – black Miss Great Britain. Singer and dancer Anita St Rose, of Trinidadian heritage but living in London, took the crown, weeks after winning the Miss Caribbean & Commonwealth title.

After returning from the Miss Universe pageant in Las Vegas, Anita became the second Miss Great Britain to resign her title. The winner's contract states that the organisation must be her sole agent for her year's reign but Anita, being a professional singer, already had an agent that she was unwilling to relinquish.

Anita's runner-up, Liz Fuller from Cardiff, took over the title and became the official 1997 winner. She would also go on to become an instrumental part of the Miss Great Britain story herself.

Runner-up Liz Fuller took over the 1996/97 title and became a future director

1998

John Singh took a back seat for the next few years, and in 1998 a businessman by the name of Nicky Price ran a competition to find the British representative for the Miss Universe pageant. Price's contest was nothing to do with John Singh or the Miss Great Britain brand, but the history books name the winners as 'Miss Great Britain', as well as their actual title, 'Miss Great Britain Universe'.

His first winner came with a fantastic fairy-tale story that the media loved. Leilani Dowding was waiting for a friend outside The Hippodrome nightclub in London, unaware that a heat of Miss Great Britain Universe was about to take place inside.

Leilani Dowding is crowned Miss Great Britain 1998

One of the organisers walked past her, immediately spotted her potential, and suggested she joined the line-up. Leilani agreed, and not only won the heat, but also the grand final a few weeks later.

Thus she became, as the daughter of a Filipina mother and British father, the first woman of Asian ancestry to represent Great Britain in the Miss Universe pageant in Hawaii.

The experience launched a successful modelling career for Leilani, and she made her debut as a Page 3 girl in *The Sun* newspaper a year later. She was also ranked in the top 100 of the World's Sexiest Women poll by readers of *FHM* magazine.

In September 2019, Leilani joined the cast of *The Real Housewives of Cheshire*, a popular ITVBe reality show following the lives of a group of glamorous, successful women and their triumphs and tribulations.

Despite being based in LA for fifteen years, Leilani was keen to return to her British roots. The offer of the TV show was, she said, the perfect opportunity for her and her rock star partner, Billy Duffy of The Cult, to move back to the UK.

1999

Nicky Price's tenure at the pageant may have been a short one, but he made his mark on its history when he was responsible for the first ever sacking of a Miss Great Britain.

A fortnight after Nicki Lane was crowned the 1999 winner, a local newspaper received a phone call from one of the other contestants revealing that Nicki was a single mother – a fact that the beauty queen had not revealed beforehand.

Because at that time the winner of Miss Great Britain qualified for the Miss Universe pageant – which, like Miss World, specifies that all contestants must be single and without children – Nicky Price had no choice but to, in his own words, 'encourage her to resign.'

'The Miss Universe winner lives and works abroad for a year,' he explained to *The Guardian*. 'We wouldn't want to split a parent from their child, or a husband from their wife, so we say no ties allowed.'

Nicki was fourteen when she became pregnant, only realising when her school skirt wouldn't fasten at the back. 'I'd never use lack of school sex education as an excuse,' she told *The Guardian*. 'It was a case of it happening the first time, it does happen to some people.'

'The doctors said I could have him adopted,' she went on, 'but I was going to bring him up the best way I could.'

At the time of her Miss Great Britain win Nicki was studying her for A levels to become a physiotherapist, and her parents were instrumental in helping to look after little Jamie.

A press conference was called and Nicki was photographed handing over her crown and sash to her runner-up Cherie Pisani, from Clacton on Sea.

'One of the reasons I went in for Miss Great Britain is because it is every girl's dream to have their picture in the papers,' Nicki said. 'To be Miss Universe, that's every girl's dream. No matter what anyone says.'

But, as will be seen four years later, Nicki's beauty queen dream was far from over.

Nicki Lane hands over her crown to Cherie Pisani
after her resignation in 1999

2000

Michelle Walker is crowned Miss Great Britain 2000

Michelle Walker, from The Wirral, became the first Miss Great Britain of the new millennium when she took the crown at London's Stringfellows nightclub.

Her win qualified her for the Miss Model of World final, a pageant run by Turkish company Interworld and run by John Singh. Michelle beat forty worldwide finalists to the crown, thus becoming the only Miss Great Britain in history to have gone on to win an international beauty title.

She also made history later that year by becoming the first woman to compete as Miss England at the Miss World pageant in 2000.

Until 1999, the winner of the Miss United Kingdom title was the sole British representative but, following devolution of the government, the four separate nations of the UK became eligible to compete in Miss World.

Michelle became an award winning bikini bodybuilding athlete and now offers fitness and pageant training to those hoping to follow in her footsteps.

2001

John Singh's team returned to stage Miss Great Britain once again, and Michelle Evans from Colwyn Bay took the crown.

Michelle's reign passed smoothly and it wasn't until years later that she found herself on the front pages.

One of the judges at the 2014 pageant was millionaire businessman Duncan Bannatyne, the sixty-six-year-old star of the BBC's hugely successful *Dragons' Den*. During the evening he got chatting to Michelle, who was there as a guest of licence owner John Singh.

Both Duncan and Michelle were recently divorced and, soon after that evening, were pictured in the press having nights out in each other's company, looking happy and relaxed.

That is, until three months later, when the press showed photos of Duncan coming out of a London restaurant with a woman who most definitely wasn't Michelle. The lady on his arm was a stunning 36-year-old from Uzbekistan called Nigora Whitehorn whom, he later revealed, he had met at the reception of a Harley Street dental practice.

Infuriated by Duncan's casual attitude – he tweeted, 'Love is in the air!' next to a photo of him with his new girlfriend - Michelle sought to redress the balance after such public humiliation.

Texting him to ask for a contribution towards the £1,200 in childcare she had paid out while they were dating, he replied telling her 'not to cause trouble'. Michelle protested that she was just speaking the truth, whereupon he replied asking if she would 'be happy with me showing the pictures you sent me?'

'Violated' at the thought of the three lingerie-clad and naked pictures she had sent Duncan early in their relationship being shared, Michelle went to the press.

The story made the front page of the *Mail on Sunday*. 'The revenge porn dragon: Duncan Bannatyne made me send him naked photos, then threatened to show them to the world, says beauty queen who dumped him,' it read.

'I thought the betrayal and public humiliation of being cheated on was as bad as it would get', she told the newspaper, 'but then he threatened me with something so personal, I was in complete shock.'

In November 2015, Duncan entered the jungle as a contestant for ITV's *I'm A Celebrity…Get Me Out of Here*, donating his six-figure fee to the Operation Smile charity in Africa. He and Nigora became engaged the following spring, marrying in a romantic beach ceremony in Portugal in June 2017.

Michelle Evans, Miss Great Britain 2001

2002

Yana Victoria Booth was crowned Miss Great Britain 2002 and took part in the Miss Europe pageant in Lebanon, becoming a top ten finalist.

One of very few British dancers to have studied at the prestigious Bolshoi Ballet, she impressed Hollywood star Sharon Stone so much that the actress contributed $75,000 towards her time there.

But Yana's height – all six feet of her – prevented her pursuing her dream career and, in frustration at being turned down by the top dance companies, decided to enter the Kent heat of the Miss Great Britain pageant, where she hoped her height would be a virtue.

Thus it proved, and Yana, who is half-Russian on her mother's side, went on to win the Miss Great Britain final at Stringfellows nightclub, beating off competition from forty-four other contestants.

Yana Booth, Miss Great Britain 2002

Boyzone singer Keith Duffy was among the judges, and the runner-up spots went to Nicky Theobald of Bedfordshire, and Lancashire's Lisa-Marie Ousby.

Pretty Polly, the tights manufacturer, immediately spotted the potential of those thirty-seven-inch legs and signed her up for an advertising campaign, while she was in demand to tell her story on *GMTV*, *The Richard & Judy Show* and *The Big Breakfast*.

2003

The winner of the 2003 Miss Great Britain pageant proved that fairy-tales do sometimes come true.

Nicki Lane, the 1999 winner who had had the title taken from her due to her being a single mum, was now twenty-four years old and living in Reading with her son, by then aged ten, and her boyfriend.

Having studied for a fitness degree at Reading University, she was working in the town's branch of Woolworths when she heard that the Miss Great Britain organisation had dropped its rule of only allowing single women to take part. Married women and mothers were now very much welcome.

The lure to try and win back the crown she'd had to relinquish was too strong for Nicki and, without telling any of her workmates, she entered the Reading heat of the Miss Great Britain pageant.

Nor did she tell them when she won that heat, or indeed the grand final a few months later.

'I thought it was better not to tell anyone,' she said, 'Then if you win, it's a nice surprise.'

Nicki beat a huge field of fifty-seven finalists to the crown in a pageant held at London's Tantra Club, with Natalie Earl of Liverpool, and Abby Saunders from Warwickshire, as runners-up.

'This win is extra special to me because of what happened a few years ago,' she said. 'It means so much more.'

A year later, however, the fairy tale ending appeared to have soured when she reflected that she would've earned more money if she'd remained at Woolworths stacking shelves.

'I only made £1,300 in earnings as Miss Great Britain,' she told *The Northern Echo*. 'I couldn't even properly provide Christmas presents for my son.'

A spokesman for Nicky Price cryptically explained that due to Nicki taking part in an 'unauthorised photoshoot' during her reign, she had been unable to fully realise the opportunity afforded to her by winning the title.

Nicki Lane wins Miss Great Britain for the second time, with 2003 runners-up
Natalie Earl and Abby Saunders

2004

Emma Spellar, Miss Great Britain 2004

Emma Spellar from Norwich took the crown in 2004 at London's Café de Paris and, with it, a host of prizes, including a holiday in Cuba and a trip to China for the Model of the World final. Abby Saunders finished first runner-up, and Daniella Allfree third.

Emma was emotional after the crowning. 'Winning means so much because I wanted to do it for my late auntie Janette, who also once competed in Miss Great Britain,' she said. Yet nine months later she was telling the *Daily Star* of, 'My Year of Hell as Miss GB.'

Emma said she received neither of the trips she won, nor saw any sign of the £28,000 modelling contract that formed part of her prize, pointing out that she earned more money as a part-time beautician than as Miss Great Britain.

'It's been a nightmare,' wailed Emma. 'The airline that was meant to fly me out to Cuba for my holiday went bust, and I was told by the organisers that I didn't need a visa to fly to China for the Model of the World contest, even though I had been insisting for months that I did. I was told a week before departure that because I had no visa, I couldn't go. They promised me the world, but all I got were a few photoshoots and TV appearances – none of which were paid. All I've received in six months is a cheque for £1,000.' Emma said the situation was so bad that she had parted company with the Miss Great Britain organisers and returned to her beautician work in Norwich.

A Miss Great Britain spokesman refuted Emma's claims. 'The reason she didn't go to China was because she decided to take a paying job at the last minute,' he said. 'And her trip to Cuba was postponed because the airline couldn't get permission to land at Gatwick. We sent her and her boyfriend to Spain instead. The PR team has done nothing wrong and it's very unfair to blame them.'

2005

The Miss Great Britain pageant didn't take place in 2005, but owner John Singh sold the company to his nephew David, following a controversy in Zimbabwe.

He had taken his Miss Tourism World pageant to the African nation that year in an attempt to help improve the country's image, but allegedly fled without paying the $200,000 dollars due to the television company who produced the show.

2006

Miss Great Britain 2006 saw one of its biggest media storms in the history of the pageant.

The Miss Great Britain franchise was bought by businessman Robert de Keyser in 2006, in conjunction with Liz Fuller, who had won the title in 1997.

A fashion agent, de Keyser was responsible for hiring Victoria Beckham as a designer for his Rock & Republic brand of jeans. He and Liz re-launched the Miss Great Britain format by scrapping the age limit and introducing voting by both the live audience and by text message.

Misdemeanours Volume One – as well as many front page headlines – detailed the spectacular sacking of Danielle Lloyd as Miss Great Britain 2006. One of the judges that night was footballer Teddy Sheringham, and they quickly became an item. But an interview that Danielle gave to a magazine gave the impression that they had been a couple well before the actual Miss Great Britain pageant.

Danielle Lloyd, Miss Great Britain 2006

Not only that, but she posed nude for *Playboy* magazine, which broke the rules a second time.

After Robert de Keyser sacked Danielle, the shamed beauty queen appeared on *Celebrity Big Brother*, where she received further scorn from the public for the part she played in the bullying of actress Shilpa Shetty during their time in the house.

Readers of *The Sun* newspaper were invited to vote for their favourite from the original finalists to replace Danielle as Miss Great Britain, and they selected British-Indian model Preeti Desai, who had originally finished fifth in the contest.

In 2007, Danielle took Miss Great Britain Limited to court in a bid to clear her name, following a front page newspaper article – headlined 'Miss Cheat Britain!' - being linked to the pageant website.

The organisation accepted that the incriminating interview that Danielle had given to *Eve* magazine was 'untrue' and that she had not met Sheringham until after the pageant. As a result, Danielle dropped her libel claim.

In a further victory for Danielle, Liz Fuller – who took sole control from de Keyser of the Miss Great Britain organisation in 2009 – made the decision to reinstate the title to Danielle.

She told *The Sun*, 'The contest is part of Danielle's history, and ours. There was no management or guidance afterwards and she ended up in *Playboy*. If there had been a management structure behind Miss Great Britain, she could have chosen a different route.'

Danielle now shares the 2006 title on the pageant's website with Preeti Desai, who became a successful Bollywood actress.

The 2006 pageant is also notable for the fact that due to the upper age restriction being lifted, a mother and daughter competed for the first time. Forty-year-old Philippa Wood entered the line-up alongside her seventeen-year-old daughter Cressida Grant in what is considered an all-time pageant first.

2007-2008

Rachael Tennant is listed in the history books as having resigned as Miss Great Britain 2007.

The blonde from Aberdeen was working for an oil company when, on a whim, she entered the pageant online.

The final, hosted by comedian Joan Rivers, was held at London's Grosvenor Hotel, and Rachael was announced as the winner, beating *Daily Star* Page 3 model Michelle Marsh, former Miss Wales Claire Evans and future *Desperate Scousewives* star Amanda Harrington.

Rachael's victory meant that she had to pull out of that year's Miss Scotland contest – the title that she had set her heart on. She had finished third in Miss Scotland the previous year and was hoping it would be second time lucky in 2007. Her win as Miss Great Britain put paid to her eligibility to take part and she admitted that she was 'gutted'.

'I never wanted to be Miss Great Britain,' she told *The Sun*. 'I mean it was fantastic and I'll never forget it, but I only ever wanted to be Miss Scotland.'

Rachael Tennant, Miss Great Britain 2007

When Miss Great Britain organiser Robert de Keyser admitted that he was having trouble finding a suitable venue for the 2008 pageant, he invited Rachael to stay on as the current titleholder until a new contest could be organised. Rachael, still hoping to pursue her Miss Scotland dream, refused his offer and stepped down, handing the crown to her runner-up Gemma Garrett.

Gemma Garrett, Miss Great Britain 2008

'I've been honoured to have been Miss Great Britain for the past year,' she said. 'I am now thrilled to hand over my crown to my friend Gemma.'

Third place went to Clair Cooper, who went on to win the Miss Universe Great Britain title in 2009.

New titleholder Gemma quickly made a name for herself when she stood as a candidate in the Crewe & Nantwich by-election on behalf of The Miss Great Britain Party, a new political party founded by de Keyser, with the aim of making Westminster 'sexy, not sleazy'.

The majority of the party's candidates were Miss Great Britain contestants, but it was titleholder Gemma who gained the most attention.

The Belfast model – who had previously won the Miss Ulster title in 1999 – finished tenth out of the ten Crewe & Nantwich candidates, but a creditable fifth out of the twenty-six standing for Haltemprice & Howden, with 521 votes.

She gave a lively interview to the *Daily Mail*, rejecting the idea of an alliance with Gordon Brown ('Have you ever seen that man smile?'), describing David Cameron as 'hot, hot, hot', didn't recognise the name of any female politician except Margaret Thatcher, and called footballers 'cocky, overconfident and contemptuous of women.'

The Miss Great Britain Party was de-registered by the Electoral Commission a year later.

Gemma appeared on a BBC3 documentary – *Gemma Garrett: Are my Fake Breasts Safe?* – in 2012, in a bid to highlight to young women the dangers of cosmetic surgery, after doctors found that her PIP breast implants had ruptured, leaving silicone in her blood.

In 2009 Miss Great Britain boss Robert de Keyser married his fourth wife Hollie, aged twenty-five, while his company, De Keyser Fashions, went into administration with debts of several million pounds.

2009

As a result of Robert de Keyser's financial situation, he was unable to stage the 2009 final himself. The company behind the contest had made losses of £53,000 in 2006 and £62,000 in 2007.

Dave Reed, of PR company Neon Management, held the pageant instead, organising a lavish show at the Café de Paris, London. He stimulated heavy media coverage, attracting thousands of entrants before whittling them down to a final twelve.

The 2009 crown was won by Newcastle marketing director Sophie Gradon, with judges including footballer Paul Gascoigne and singer Simon Webbe from pop band Blue.

Shortly after the crowning, Liz Fuller bought the Miss Great Britain franchise from Robert de Keyser and inherited Sophie as her first winner. It proved to be not the easiest of starts when a row erupted on social media concerning a penalty train fare the beauty queen had incurred while attending a photo shoot for a skincare brand.

The skincare company had liaised directly with Sophie as to which train times suited her, and had booked and paid for the tickets. However, when Sophie decided to board an earlier more expensive train, she was fined £70 by the ticket inspector. She passed the fine on to the Miss Great Britain head office and was incensed when they refused to pay it.

A statement on the Miss Great Britain website read, 'Sophie Gradon will not be attending the final on Saturday. She has been demanding that Miss GB pay a train fare she incurred because she boarded the wrong train. Miss GB cannot encourage irresponsible behaviour and will not be paying any train fines, parking fines, library fines, etc.'

Sophie, in response, told the *Daily Star Sunday*, 'I'm absolutely disgusted to find out that the fine wouldn't be paid. I got a court summons from the rail company and now I'm being asked to pay £150. I did so much work as Miss Great Britain and I thought they would pay my train ticket.'

New owner Liz Fuller told the newspaper that, 'Sophie will not be welcome at the 2010 ceremony as she has created a lot of bad feelings and has behaved in a very irresponsible way. As far as we know, she just couldn't be bothered to get on the right train.'

As for allegations from Sophie that no opportunities had been created for her, Liz was happy to put the record straight. 'That was unfair of Sophie. We got her photo shoots, personal appearances and a three-page spread in *OK!* Magazine. We would've got her more if she hadn't tried to abuse her position, asking the ticket inspector, "Don't you know who I am?" and saying that Miss Great Britain should travel for free.'

Sophie even went so far as to sue the organisation in court over the £70 fine. She lost her case.

'What is it with these girls that they believe nothing is their fault?' Liz Fuller asked.

Speaking to the author a few years ago, Sophie admitted that she had been 'young and naïve' during her reign, and that she 'probably did get on the wrong train – I'm hopeless at organising myself.'

Sophie Gradon, Miss Great Britain 2009

Of her year as Miss Great Britain, she said, 'Dave Reed at Neon Management was a great guy, but had a different vision of how he saw the winner. He wanted to go more down the glamour route.

'I did a shoot with *Nuts* magazine with some beautiful lingerie, and had agreed not to go topless. In the shoot

I was coerced into doing 'implied topless' - my boobs were covered, often with my hands. Needless to say all the pics in the mag were of me with my bra off and the shots of me with my bra on were simply the 'warm up'. I made the mistake of reading the readers' comments online – 'skinny', 'fat', 'ugly', 'looks like a man in drag' – and it made me near suicidal, it made me hate myself.'

Sophie says that Liz Fuller taking over the franchise was 'like a breath of fresh air', yet she found that 'being treated like a piece of meat at functions, someone to be looked at and touched, and for remarks to made about my looks, made me realise that I didn't have the thick skin necessary to be a beauty queen or model.

'I decided then that I no longer wanted to be judged simply on how I looked, and I returned to my studies and a more normal life. After all, I have a brain, I have feelings – people seem to forget that!'

In 2016, Sophie joined the cast of ITV2's *Love Island*, a reality show in which single men and women are flown out to a luxury villa in Mallorca, where cameras capture every second of budding romances and furious rows.

Sophie paired up with Welsh barman Tom Powell and, despite their tempestuous relationship on the show, they stayed together as a couple after leaving the villa, before finally splitting later that year.

In the most tragic chapter of the Miss Great Britain pageant, Sophie made headlines all over the world in June 2018, when she was found dead in her parents' house in Ponteland, Northumberland.

At just thirty-two years old, Sophie had taken a fatal combination of cocaine and alcohol and, according to the coroner's report, chosen to end her life.

Sophie had suffered from depression before her appearance on *Love Island,* but in a radio interview just months before her death she had spoken about her anxiety being exacerbated by an onslaught of online bullying and what she perceived was a lack of after-care from the TV production team.

'The negative comments were horrific,' she said. 'It can really get into your mind and affect you.' With tragic prophecy, Sophie continued, 'The harsh reality is that it can end up with that person taking their own life. Can you imagine being responsible for that?'

Sophie was laid to rest at a funeral service in her hometown, while *Love Island* dedicated an episode of the

2018 series to her memory.

During our conversations in 2015, Sophie told me she had auctioned off her Miss Great Britain crown. 'I gave it to a wonderful charity that sends children diagnosed with cancer to a retreat with their family. The money I raised was able to send a family of five away. I'm just happy that I could at least do that.'

2010

Liz Fuller had her work cut out in 2010 when it came to damage limitation in the media. The pageant was hit with a slew of unwelcome publicity involving some of the contestants even before the final had begun.

The adverse media coverage began with the sacking of the winner of the Central London heat. Lora Jayne Nuttall was stripped of her sash hours after winning when organisers discovered that one of the judges, Big Brother contestant Rex Newmark, was a former boyfriend, and was friends with another, TV fashion expert Julian Bennett.

Liz Fuller declared that she was considering all-female judging panels in future, and that the Central London heat would be run again, admitting to *The Sun,* 'It was a bad start for someone who had promised to reintroduce ethics to the pageant.'

Then, came the story of twenty-seven year old Laura Anness, who arguably goes down in history as the only beauty queen to be stripped of two titles within as many months. Disqualified from the Miss England pageant for lying about her age, she won the Plymouth heat of Miss Great Britain before being exposed by the *Daily Express* as a former prostitute.

The article alleged that she had posed topless for a Sunday newspaper in 1999 and revealed how she had worked in a massage parlour at the age of sixteen, earning up to £400 a week.

'They told me I'd have to do extras,' she told the reporter at the time. 'I thought I'd give it a try.'

'I'm shocked,' Liz Fuller told the *Express* after she had stripped Laura of her title. 'Miss GB must be a good role model for female society.'

But the drama was far from over. Shirlena Johnson had already competed in three heats of the 2010 pageant and each time had given her age as twenty-eight.

However, the singer's true age of thirty was uncovered when Shirlena's audition for ITV's *The X Factor* talent show was shown that summer. Performing a bizarre version of Duffy's hit single *Mercy*, Shirlena was shown clawing at the floor and growling at the camera.

Once more, Liz Fuller was forced to step in and ban her from the pageant, while at pains to explain that the decision was purely down to age.

The stress of facing one drama after another made Liz ill with suspected pneumonia just before the final but, as she told *The Sun*, 'I ignored it, I couldn't be ill.'

Amy Carrier, Miss Great Britain 2010, with runners-up Lisa Lazarus (L) and Gina Basham (R)

Former Miss World Rosanna Davison was among the judges for the lavish black-tie grand final in Weston-Super-Mare, yet even the show itself was beset with problems.

Liz told *The Sun*, 'Just as I was announcing the final twelve, a producer ran to the side of the stage and told me he had forgotten to include the winner of the public phone and text vote. So, rather embarrassingly, we had to have a top thirteen and, even though we had made her a finalist as well, I realised I would have to refund her family the £2,000 they had spent on voting for her.'

Even with the beleaguered contest safely over, poor Liz was to face yet more acrimony.

Hours after Liverpool law student Amy Carrier took the crown – beating former Miss Universe UK Lisa Lazarus into second place – irate fans, together with losing contestants and their families, vented their disgust online, accusing Liz Fuller of fixing the result.

An article in the *Daily Star Sunday* reported that one claimed: 'Yes, Liz Fuller, your competition is a BIG FIX. Liz Fuller picked the top twenty-five, not the judges. Liz Fuller picked the winner.'

Another raged, 'Absolute joke, this competition! I was there and I heard the organisers say that the judges' opinions were not needed and that the organisers would pick the winner.'

Liz refuted these claims in the strongest possible terms. 'The top twenty-five were chosen by the judges in a pre-interview judging session that lasted over five hours,' she said. 'Each of the five judges met each contestant for five to ten minutes, asking them important questions and allowing their Facebook pages to be studied in order to assess their character.

'The interview process went on until 1am because it was so important for us to find a great ambassador and a genuinely nice girl. We didn't want another beautiful girl with an ugly personality.'

She reiterated these views in the *Daily Star*. 'I've had loads of abuse since the results. But the comments are coming from sore losers and bitches. Some of them may be confused as to why certain girls didn't make the final twelve. We weren't looking for just beauty, but girls who had character too. I wanted a girl who the others could look up to. Amy was the perfect winner.'

'I saw some sights on some of their Facebook pages,' she said. 'There were pictures of some getting drunk, status updates with swearing, details of the men they've slept with. That is not the sort of girl we were looking for.'

Liz had been dealt a blow three months earlier, when a deal she was about to strike with Channel 5 to screen the pageant fell through, after TV executives decided to take the *Big Brother* programme instead after it was dropped by Channel 4.

Despite the Weston-Super-Mare final being profitable, and having been featured on many TV shows and in the press, Liz Fuller decided enough was enough and she sold the company at the beginning of 2011.

Under the headline, *Miss GBH*, Liz gave her story to *The Sun* as to how her dream of reviving the pageant turned into fourteen months of hell.

In the piece she wrote herself, she said, 'I did meet some beautiful and talented girls, but I also met a never-ending parade of girls whose ultimate aspiration is instant fame or WAGdom. Most had two things in common: Jordan was their heroine, and they were bad losers.'

Describing the girls who had posed topless, enjoyed relationships with the judges, lied about their ages, and spats with family members unhappy at the results, she said, 'It sounds like '*Carry On Up The Catwalk*', but the consequences have been serious. It dented my belief in others and my sense of fair play.

'One PR company even asked me to fix the result so that a girlfriend of a sportsman on their books would win. Those fourteen months cost me my health and any chance of a personal life or serious relationship. It also cost me my peace of mind.

'I now know how the beauty industry works – inside and out – and it's not an experience I want to repeat.'

Liz told the author, 'I was a judge or presenter at every Miss Great Britain pageant from 1999 to 2006, so I saw and heard just as many issues as I went through; what shocked me was finding out who was causing these issues. To be told that one of the sweetest of girls had a background in prostitution was such a shock. It proves how important background checks on the contestants are.

'It's also easy for a contestant to put on an act or put forward a certain persona for the judges. An organisation or judge has to be able to evaluate and analyse this.'

Liz handed the Miss Great Britain licence back to David Singh and left to go and live in the States, where she forged a successful career as an actress and TV presenter. She is now the CEO of Miss British Empire, a pageant she launched in 2011 and joint-director of the Miss World America contest, to choose the USA's representative to Miss World.

American former model and professional matchmaker Wendy Seinturier had been working alongside Liz Fuller as the pageant's Etiquette and Runway coach, and bought the licence from the Singhs.

However, when she sacked Miss York City, Charlotte Campbell, for posing for 'implied nude' photos, she faced a storm of undesired press attention and stepped down as CEO.

Yet again, the Miss Great Britain ship was suddenly left without an anchor, and there was no pageant held in either 2011 or 2012.

2013

Salvation came in the form of another former beauty queen. Kate Solomons-Freakley had been both a Miss England runner-up and host when, in 2005, she founded ModelZed (since rebranded as The Kreative Group), a promotion and events agency based in her home town of Leicester.

Kate had dreamed of running a major beauty pageant and her chance came in 2012 when she and colleague Jemma Simmonds took on the franchise for Miss Great Britain from David Singh, with the winner representing the country in the final of the Miss Tourism World pageant.

The Athena in Leicester, a former art deco cinema and now a conferencing and banqueting venue, has hosted the Miss Great Britain every year since, and that first year saw Sheffield's Ashley Powell take the crown.

Ashley Powell, Miss Great Britain 2013

Ashley went on to further success in 2017 when she was crowned Miss International UK, Miss International Europe, and finished in the top eight of the Miss International final in Japan. She also won the Miss Scuba UK title in 2019, in doing so becoming one of the most decorated Miss Great Britain winners of the modern era.

2014

Shelby Tribble faced the worst kind of insult after she had been crowned Miss Great Britain 2014. Czech website *Extra.cz* claimed that Shelby was not beautiful enough to have won the title, printing her photo with her face pixelated out.

It was a cruel blow for the stunning twenty-one-year-old from Plymouth, who had already revealed that she had been painfully shy and subjected to constant bullying at school.

Shelby gained huge support from her online fans after the attack, and had the last laugh by becoming a household name as a star on ITVBe's *The Only Way is Essex*, joining the cast in 2018 for a year and quickly establishing herself as a fan favourite.

Shelby Tribble Miss Great Britain 2014

Zara Holland (above centre) the original winner in 2015. She was replaced by runner-up Deone Robertson (below) after Zara's appearance on ITV's 'Love Island'

2015

Zara Holland was crowned Miss Great Britain 2015 in front of an audience which included former titleholders, invited to commemorate the 70th anniversary of the country's longest running beauty pageant.

Fellow judge Danielle Lloyd had no idea that the contestant she would help select that night would replace her as the most notorious beauty queen of the modern era, nor that she would join her as only the second Miss Great Britain to be sacked.

But following Zara's very public display of ardour on ITV's *Love Island* the following summer – where she was seen having sex with a housemate on the day of his arrival – she was de-crowned while still a contestant on the show.

'Following recent actions within the ITV show *Love Island*,' ModelZed's statement said, 'it is with deep regret that we, the Miss Great Britain organisation, have to announce that Zara Holland has been formally de-crowned as Miss Great Britain 2015/16.'

They would, they announced, be crowning first runner-up, Deone Robertson of North Lanarkshire – a former Miss Galaxy Scotland and Miss European – as the new Miss Great Britain for the remaining three months of the reign.

Social media sites as Facebook and Twitter were still in their infancy when Danielle Lloyd lost her crown in 2004, but news of Zara's de-crowning made headlines in every newspaper in the country, while websites all over the world reported the controversy, making her the most talked-about and infamous beauty queen of the internet age.

Many social media users accused the Miss Great Britain organisation of being old fashioned, slamming them for shaming Zara for making 'adult decisions'. A petition to get her crown reinstated received over 21,000 online signatures.

Zara was heartbroken at losing the title she had worked so hard for.

'I did Miss Great Britain because I wanted to,' she said. 'I put in the time and commitment and effort, and I won. Now I made just one silly, stupid mistake of being in the moment and it's ruined everything.'

The moral argument of the actions of both Zara and the Miss Great Britain office raged back and forth across the press, media, television and online. *The Daily Telegraph* political editor Michael Wilkinson weighed in with an article calling the Miss GB office a 'disgrace' for priding themselves on being a platform for women's rights, yet shaming Zara by de-crowning her, while ITV's Lorraine Kelly gave her no sympathy when she invited her onto her morning show.

Meanwhile, Kate herself was subjected to abuse on a huge scale.

'It was absolutely horrendous,' she recalled. 'I underestimated how many people would be so supportive of Zara and deem what she did as perfectly acceptable. I had never been so bullied – receiving emails and messages of hate, and phone calls at all hours.

'People thought we were a big, corporate organisation with a firm to handle the PR, but it's just me and Jemma, two thirty-something married mums. We had spent the past four years working hard to turn the pageant around to change the lads' mags stereotypical image of Miss Great Britain, but Zara's actions undid it all.'

The denouement came when ITV's popular daytime show *Loose Women* invited both Zara and her successor, Deone Robertson, onto the show to discuss what had happened.

Zara criticised Deone for not refusing the crown in a show of solidarity, and blamed the Miss GB organisation for not waiting until she had left *Love Island* to release the news of her de-crowning.

But the *Loose Women* panellists – including Andrea Maclean and Katie Price – showed little mercy or sympathy towards her and the general consensus was that this appearance had put a full stop under the whole sorry saga.

Zara was not without genuine remorse, though, vowing to 'count to ten and think before I do things,' but adding that the whole experience 'had made me a stronger person.'

When Ursula Carlton from Aberdeen was crowned Miss Great Britain 2016, Zara was of course not present to hand over her title, but had some wise words for the new winner. 'Ursula needs to steer clear of reality shows,' she said. 'It's not a good idea if you want to keep your title. Reality bites, as they say.'

2016

The Miss Great Britain title remained in Scotland, when Deone Robertson handed the crown to Aberdeen's Ursula Carlton, in a pageant judged by singer and actor Jake Quickenden and model Cally-Jane Beech.

Ursula, who worked as a Disney princess, became the only Miss Great Britain to land a three-page spread in the prestigious *Lady* magazine.

Ursula Carlton, Miss Great Britain 2016

2017

Saffron Rose Hart landed Hull's second Miss Great Britain crown in three years, and vowed to stay away from reality television.

Since ModelZed – now rebranded as Kreative - took over the Miss Great Britain franchise in 2013, the winner qualified for the Miss Tourism World pageant, another owned by David Singh.

Saffron Rose Hart, Miss Great Britain 2017

British contestants had done well in the pageant to date, with both Ashley Powell and Shelby Tribble making the top five. And when Saffron Hart flew to Malaysia for the pageant, she was delighted to keep the flag flying by also being announced on stage as a top five finalist.

Yet, to her shock, the presenters then announced that due to a technical error, they would be announcing the top five again.

In this second announcement, Saffron didn't make the cut, and faced the humiliation of having to walk off stage.

'It was so amateur and unprofessional,' she told the *Mail on Sunday*. 'What an embarrassment.'

Saffron bounced back and during the course of her reign appeared as a spokesperson for pageants with Piers Morgan on *Good Morning Britain*, debating a range of topics including *Love Island* and the Miss America bikini ban.

She is also the official mentor and trainer to Miss Great Britain contestants, who take great comfort and inspiration from her words of advice and encouragement.

2018/2019

It was third time lucky for Kobi-Jean Cole when she was crowned Miss Great Britain 2018, and in doing so becoming the first ever winner from Bristol.

Kobi-Jean Cole, Miss Great Britain 2018/19

Kobi-Jean competed in the Miss Tourism World final in Croatia and was then chosen to launch the Purple Poppy Appeal, an initiative spear-headed by the War Horse Memorial Trust to raise awareness of the work and sacrifices made by horses and other animals who served during the war.

Kobi-Jean had the honour of launching the 2019 Appeal at the Animals in War memorial statue in London's Hyde Park in front of the British press, while wearing a stunning cloak made up of thousands of knitted purple poppies sent in from kind-hearted supporters from all over the world.

With the 2019 Miss Great Britain pageant cancelled due to owner David Singh postponing his Miss Tourism World final, Kobi-Jean was able to reign for seventeen months before handing over her crown at the glittering 75th anniversary event in February 2020.

2020

The 75th anniversary of the Miss Great Britain pageant was commemorated in a very special way.

As well as choosing the Diamond Celebration winner, the team behind the pageant launched the first ever Ms Great Britain title, for those over the regular age limit of twenty-seven.

The inaugural Ms Great Britain pageant was designed for women aged twenty-eight and above, of any marital status or background. The move proved instantly popular, attracting the crème de la crème of those who had 'aged out' of mainstream pageants.

Fittingly, the very first Ms Great Britain crown went to April Banbury, who had twice competed in Miss Great Britain – in 2014 and 2016 - and had twice finished runner-up.

April, who competed in the first edition of *The Bachelor UK* in 2011, starring rugby legend Gavin Henson, was a thirty-year old fashion designer who had won plaudits for featuring models with Downs Syndrome during her shows at London Fashion Week.

Competing alongside April was a plethora of former national titleholders, including Zoe Salmon, from Belfast.

Zoe had been Miss Northern Ireland 1999, but was best known as a BBC *Blue Peter* presenter and contestant on ITV's *Dancing On Ice*.

Joining April on the winners' rostrum was the 75th Miss Great Britain, Jen Atkin, from Grimsby.

Jen, aged twenty-six, who had finished first runner-up in the 2018 Miss England pageant, was a successful country singer and her new single was released the week after her Miss Great Britain win.

What really won the hearts of the judges, though, was the story of her incredible weight loss: two years earlier Jen had weighed seventeen stones, but her sheer willpower and determination meant that by the time she walked onto the Miss Great Britain stage she had lost an astonishing eight stones in weight.

Her story piqued an interest in pageants not seen in the mainstream press for years, and Jen's epic weight-loss and Miss Great Britain victory was reported in newspapers from as far afield as Turkey, Malaysia, Australia and the USA.

2020 winners: April Banbury (left) the first ever Ms Great Britain,
with Jen Atkin, the 75th Miss Great Britain

She also appeared as a guest on ITV's *Good Morning Britain*, where she was happy to put the record straight on reports that her fiancé had left her due to her former size.

'That's not the case,' said Jen. 'We are still friends and I am now happily married to someone else.'

She went on to say that she felt her personality won her the Miss Great Britain crown. 'I wasn't the prettiest girl there and I was probably the biggest there too, but I was chosen because I have a good personality and an inspiring story.'

Jen became the first married winner of the Miss Great Britain pageant since Debbie Greenwood in 1984.

The Miss Great Britain pageant has seen some tumultuous times in its seventy-five-year-old existence, but has managed to see off the formidable opposition of court cases, television bans, front page scandals and several changes of ownership. It has survived and flourished and moved with the times, regaining its status as one of the most prestigious pageants in the country.

As we salute the Diamond Anniversary of the Miss Great Britain pageant – and the thousands of women who have competed up and down the country in heats and finals since 1945 – we raise a glass to the next seventy-five years of Britain's favourite beauty pageant.

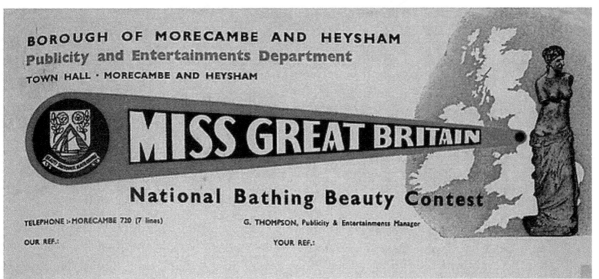

CPSIA information can be obtained
at www.ICGtesting.com
Printed in the USA
BVHW021259141022
649460BV00020B/1143

9 781913 071790